LOVE'S KEEPSAKE

First published 2024

Copyright © Robert B Findlay 2024

The right of Robert B Findlay to be identified as the author of this work has been asserted in accordance with the Copyright, Designs & Patents Act 1988.

All rights reserved. No part of this book may be reproduced, stored in a retrieval system, or transmitted in any form or by any means, digital, electronic, electrostatic, magnetic tape, mechanical, photocopying, recording or otherwise, without the written permission of the copyright holder.

Published under licence by Brown Dog Books and
The Self-Publishing Partnership Ltd, 10b Greenway Farm, Bath Rd, Wick,
nr. Bath BS30 5RL, UK

www.selfpublishingpartnership.co.uk

ISBN printed book: 978-1-83952-830-9
ISBN e-book: 978-1-83952-831-6

Cover design by Andrew Prescott
Internal design by Andrew Easton

Printed and bound in the UK

This book is printed on FSC® certified paper

LOVE'S KEEPSAKE

ROBERT B FINDLAY

LOVE'S KEEPSAKE

My father was named after the Scottish poet Robert Burns, so when I eventually arrived on 25 January 1951, I too had to have that name! It is not surprising then that I took an interest in poetry from an early age and when I was sixteen I was encouraged to keep writing by a friend of W. H. Auden who had read some of my work. Almost fifty years on I am still using poetry to express my feelings or speak out against social injustice.

I was inspired and influenced by both British and American poets and songwriters ranging from the Liverpool poets through to e e cummings, Bob Dylan and Simon and Garfunkel.

As a non-conformist, I challenge boundaries and assumptions, refusing to have a label or category. So there is no one particular style I prefer; each piece of work dictates how it wishes to appear on the page. The language I use is direct in order to convey the meaning and emotions within and between the words. My work stretches from the romantic to the protest and I firmly believe my namesake would have approved!

Love's Keepsake is a collection of my poetry and lyrics which stem from the 1980s to the present. The majority of them have not been published before. There are a few taken from previously published poetry pamphlets and material taken from my two Facebook pages. I continue to write under the name: Robert B. Findlay.*

I have had many discussions over the years about poetic licence and questions about content. It is a fact that the poetry does contain personal feelings towards people and events, however, I would advise against making assumptions about a specific poem unless it is glaring obvious what or whom I am writing about.

My greatest hope is that you will enjoy reading my work as much as I enjoyed writing it.

* I prefer to work under my birth name (as above) as opposed to my legal name of Robert B Williams-Findlay

CONTENT

Political Poems and Snippets — 15

1. House of Cards — 16
2. They Know What They Do — 17
3. Spirit of 45 — 18
4. The Spectre — 18
5. Who are these people? — 19
6. Out Of Sight And Out Of Mind — 20
7. New Year — 21
8. Embers — 21
9. 1984 — 22
10. Toffee Nose — 23
11. Tory Minister of Culture — 24
12. Post Capitalism — 24
13. Cameron — 24
14. Let's spell it out — 25
15. My moment — 25
16. Eye to Eye — 26
17. Say that again? — 27
18. Lost Days — 27
19. Two Sides — 28
20. Top Gear — 28
21. Comrade — 29

22.	Disability charities	30
23.	Joe Cocker	31
24.	Poem for Liz	31
25.	Waiting	32
26.	White Rabbit	32
27.	Sense of Power	34
28.	Disquiet	35
29.	Just another scrounger	35
30.	Ms Whiplash	36
31.	Disability Pride	36
32.	Know Our Place	38
33.	Cathy Can't	38
34.	Material Failure	39

Sentiments and Memories to Treasure — 40

35.	Love's Keepsake	41
36.	Days of Sleepless Nights	42
37.	Lovelorn	43
38.	You'll need to ask yourself why	43
39.	When I tell you	44
40.	Mourning Memories Passing	45
41.	Menu	45
42.	I'll never lose you	46
43.	Forbidden Fruits	47
44.	A miracle or two	48
45.	I don't get	49
46.	Duo	50
47.	You know I'm into you	50
48.	When	52
49.	Promised Land	53

50.	Pause for Thought	54
51.	When We	54
52.	If You Want to Hear Good News	55
53.	If I Were	56
54.	Fishing	57
55.	Spades	57
56.	The More You Deny It	57
57.	I'm Thinking	58
58.	If I Could....Would I?	58
59.	Thief	59
60.	Missing you	60
61.	Thinking once again about what might have been	60
62.	I Promised	61
63.	Love Poem	62
64.	I would	62
65.	U r	63
66.	Distance	64
67.	Between	64
68.	Caught	64
69.	What You Are	65
70.	Agenda	65

Ancient and Modern — 66

71.	Against the odds	67
72.	Bridges start to burn	67
73.	Shaun the sheep	68
74.	Why?	68
75.	Our Name: It Is Invisible	69
76.	Little Step Back	70
77.	The Beauty	71

78.	Rain	71
79.	No Doubt	72
80.	Ever	73
81.	Intoxicated	74
82.	Land Of Make Believe	74
83.	No Chance	75
84.	You Are	76
85.	Melt	77
86.	No One Breaks My Heart, Like Me	77
87.	We're on the same page	79
88.	What I am to you	80
89.	Empty Shore	82
90.	Endless Day	83
91.	Dipping my toe in the water	84
92.	Brighton	85
93.	Welcome to Britain	86
94.	Too painful	87
95.	I just want to love you	87
96.	Once	88
97.	There are things	89
98.	Lost in thought	89
99.	When you are with me	90
100.	Waves	91
101.	Dear Life	92
102.	The Scales Weigh Heavy	93
103.	Caught Up in Someone's Dreams	93
104.	Proximity	94
105.	Tea and Sympathy	95
106.	You and I	96
107.	Like an Eagle That's Taken Wing	96

108. Within the Silence	97
109. You're Wondering	98
110. Outside Our Comfort Zone	99
111. Critical Acclaim – Offer a Little Light	99

Something Old, Something New — 101

112. Life	102
113. For the Canny, Nothing New	102
114. Nothing Obvious	103
115. Drift Away	104
116. Habit	104
117. Looking Sheepish	105
118. When Dreams Come True	106
119. Body Fascism	106
120. Edge	107
121. Mermaid	108
122. Train	108
123. No Recollection	109
124. Expectations	110
125. That Time After Midnight	111
126. Never Know	111
127. Perhaps	112
128. Current Times Are Shocking	112
129. I Can't Find Myself	114
130. There Are Still Words	115
131. After The Storm	115
132. Bosnia: Holocaust II	116
133. Mirror Girl	117
134. Taken	118
135. The Keeper of My Heart	119

136. Love Still Endures	119
137. Memories Caught	120
138. You Turn Away	120
139. Off Guard	121
140. Never Mind	122
141. Remembering Little Big Horn	123
142. Past Tense	124
143. The Magpie	124
144. First Time	125
145. The Family	126
146. Maybe	126
147. Hear is the News	127
148. Use your Mobile	128
149. So Many People	128
150. Miss You	130
151. Making Sense of Contradictions	131
152. Display	131

Love, Life, and Loneliness — 132

153. It's in the Moment	133
154. Secrets	133
155. Treading Water	135
156. Between a Rock and a Hard Place	136
157. Minute to Minute	136
158. Looking for Answers	137
159. Looks as if the Die's Already Been Cast	138
160. Ghosts from the Past	139
161. Man Made	139
162. Rising Tide	140
163. If You Were to be Believed	140

164.	Praxis	141
165.	Reflecting Upon Yesterday	142
166.	The Words on the Page Were Like a Knife to the Heart	143
167.	It's Like the Itch You Can Never Reach	143
168.	From Tiergartenstrasse to Treloar	144
169.	Where Do You Begin?	145
170.	Sean	145
171.	When Time Stood Frozen to the Spot	146
172.	Knowledge	147
173.	True Colours	147
174.	Intimidation	148
175.	What Might Have Been	149
176.	I Am Not	149
177.	The Love Affair	150
178.	Alternate Reality	151
179.	Aftermath	151
180.	Discourse	152
181.	Austerity	152
182.	2023	153
183.	Nothing to fear	153
184.	Self-respect	154
185.	Lambs to Slaughter	155
186.	Partners in Crime	155
187.	Images of Kati	156
188.	Satanic Verse	157
189.	The Same Old Story in a Different Disguise	157
190.	Passive Resistance	158
191.	If Only	159
192.	Children in Need: the Saville Row	160
193.	There Are Things to Forget	161

Words and Memories Together Forever

194. This is Albion	163
195. Socialism	163
196. I Wish I Could be in Denial	164
197. Sophie Ann	165
198. Peter Tosh	166
199. Thank You	168
200. Take No Prisoners	170
201. Badge of Shame	171
202. Rollercoaster	172
203. Circle of Love	173
204. Empathy	174
205. Old Man	175
206. Revolution Betrayed	176
207. Santiago 1973	177
208. An Observation	178
209. There's Nothing Unusual	178
210. Empty Rooms and Meaningless Smiles	180
211. Understanding	181
212. Baghdad 2004	182
213. All of a Sudden	184
214. Waiting for the Man	185
215. It's That Time Again	185
216. Flotsam and Jetsam	186
217. There Was a Time Before You	187
218. There's Nothing	188
219. The Things I Do	188
220. Out of the Blue	189

# POLITICAL POEMS AND SNIPPETS

LOVE'S KEEPSAKE

House of Cards

The writing's writ large
Upon a nearby wall
Your days are numbered
And it won't be long before
We see your house of cards fall

Can't expect the cavalry
To come charging over
Some distant hill
To save your sorry hide
From the people's will

Now the table's turned;
Not another ace to play,
Friends have all folded,
You're on your own, Jack;
This time you're going to pay

Thought you had your cards
Tight up against your chest,
But there's more than one way
To read a desperate hand;
So you're going down with the rest

The writing's writ large
Upon a nearby wall
Your days are numbered
And it won't be long before
We see your house of cards fall.

If I were a betting woman
I'd be willing to raise the stakes
And make you sweat awhile
Hoping you'd have time to recall
All your silly, stupid little mistakes

But I have no desire to gamble,
This isn't my game to lose,
Not when all the cards
Are clearly stacked against you;
Why put myself in your shoes?

They Know What They Do

They are skilled in pulling the wool over your eyes
Stitching together a patchwork of deceit and lies
Do you think they care how many have died?
Outcome the same whether a natural death or suicide

Do you think they worry over your fate;
Their only concern is reducing the welfare state
Of course they have no regard for human rights
When they have making profit in their sights

Not a question of failing to comprehend
Today these people see no need to pretend
They are out to smash all of our gains
And they care not how much it pains
Don't be fooled by liberal democracy

It was never established for you or me
Houses of Parliament you see
Protect the interests of the bourgeoisie

Spirit of '45

What will it take to keep alive
The hope that flamed the Spirit of '45?
From the ashes of a Europe torn apart
Rose a hope to strengthen the heart.
A desire to put an end to poverty,
To build a future based upon equality.
Today, we need to see that flame burn
And assist the Spirit of 45 to return
Make sure we'll never see the jackboot again
Or allow our people to labour in vain.

The Spectre

People can't eat bullets or bombs
Yet Cameron provides a diet of hate
The ruling class wants to force our retreat
By putting goons in uniform on the street

The terror isn't being housed in Syria or Baghdad central
Look no further than sordid places like News International
For it's the likes of Murdoch and his fellow mogul scum
Who are gearing up to put our class on the run

The spectre that appears to be on the rise
Is still lurking beneath a fake democratic disguise
But take care; if we don't prepare and organise,
The iron fist in the velvet will soon be before our eyes.

Who Are These People?

With stones in their hands and hearts
They judge what they can't comprehend
With words of ignorance and stupidity
They go out of their way to offend

With the media at their side
They denounce those who dare speak
With untold power in buckets
They pour down on those who are weak

With axes to grind and tongues to wag
They administer the iron first in a velvet glove
With stones in their hands and hearts
They screw rather than make love

LOVE'S KEEPSAKE

Out of Sight and Out of Mind

Out of sight and out of mind
Through the guilt of humankind
The children you'll never see
Those born of a world of misery!

I'll tell you of their crime
To pass nine months of gestation time –
Be sentenced to a lifetime of hell
Locked in an orphanage-prison cell

Here, the sun never shines,
And there's nothing to occupy minds
Little ones left to slowly decay –
Who'll take this torment away?

But what hope for that child
Deformed, now so 'crippled' and wild?
Will it forever be cast to one side
As the do-gooders turn back the tide?

As we start to use our voices,
Demanding the right to make choices,
Our words must reach out worldwide
To touch those they still hide!

From Birmingham to Bucharest
The struggle continues without rest
Till all of these children are free
There will be no liberation from disability!

New Year

When Fire called upon Oil to unite
It was a simple ploy to make Oil ignite
So let's get something quite clear
At the start of the New Year
You and I are chalk and cheese
We'd never mix with ease
Never lie together in the same bed
Are we clear, Mr Ed?

Embers

For people like Abdullah Kurdi

As the dying embers of the year
Struggle to burn, give off heat,
Who will shed a mournful tear
For the children we'll never meet
Lost out from some distant shore?

Who will recall a father's grief
Or the vision of a mother's broken heart?
Will our memories be but brief
As we await a new year to start?

War doesn't measure in terms of days
Or employ tables to work out its price,
War kills in so many different ways
While always demanding a sacrifice

The talk this week is of love and peace
And about the birth of a Messiah
Of wonders that will never cease
But I look deep into the embers of a fire.

1984

If Winston had been a cripple in 1984
He'd have to wait a decade before
Big Brother's double-speak
Left him completely up the creek
'Cos we all know that rights
Are never granted by a bunch of shites!

LOVE'S KEEPSAKE

Toffee Nose

Have you ever been revolted
By someone's late night take-away
Lying spewed in the gutter?

Have you heard about the tweet
The shameless shite McVey
Posted during the '96 service yesterday?

The puke was the result of
Foolish self-indulgence by a drunk
At the end of the day

The tweet was a product of
a self-indulgent skank
Whose antics are enough to make you puke
The shameless shite McVey
Posted during the 96 service yesteday

The puke was the result of
Foolish self-indulgence by a drunk
At the end of the day
The tweet was a product of
a self-indulgent skank
Who's antics are enough to make you puke

Tory Minister of Culture

That lady has no culture
She doesn't have any class
Makes her ill-gotten living
From selling her bloody arse

Nothing novel about her
She's not a picture to behold
Certainly isn't something to treasure
Just a liar now out in the cold

Post-Capitalism

I'm dreaming of a tomorrow
Beyond the confines of your expectations
Past the limitations you impose
I wasn't fashioned in your image nor touched by
The falsehood of the Gods you worship

Cameron

He says he's a man of the people
That he's on everybody's side
And when a big decision has to be made
He'll let the people decide

Do we cut hours or jobs
Introduce zero hours galore
Yes, he's a real man of the people
And you've heard it all before

Let's Spell It Out

T is for Tories, the nasty makers of tears
H is for hateful bigots who prey on people's fears
A is for arrogant arseholes sitting on the front bench
T is also for the thugs who are creating an awful stench
C is for Conservatives who spread this government's lies
H is for hopelessness seen in people's haunted eyes
E is for evil benefit reforms disabled people grew to despise
R is for revolution, the best method for saying our good byes

My Moment

By way of an explanation
Do not see my silence as a rejection
As an indication of my fear of confrontation
It is merely a moment in which I exist
In another place and time:
Where I can recharge my batteries in order to rejoin the struggle

LOVE'S KEEPSAKE

Eye to Eye

They keep telling us lies
But I can see by your eyes
That you want compromise
As it is the best we can do

If I were an ocean
I could make waves for you
But I have this notion
You would prefer a calm sea

Yes, we are chalk and cheese,
And no matter how I try to please
There is no way I can deny
We keep failing to see eye to eye

I would describe it as betrayal
You view it as diplomacy
I want to fight tooth and nail
But the towel is already down

If I were an ocean
You would be a distant shore
Without a trace of emotion
We would stand eye to eye

Say That Again?

I made my point sharply
I went to pieces when I snapped
Came up short before the end
Went over the top joining the other side
Felt a fool, but he didn't mind
I hesitated with a pregnant pause
Came full circle in a roundabout way

Lost Days

started off in the vanguard
but fell back to the rear
as the momentum for change
suddenly hit reverse gear

with the opium of the masses
donning a freshly painted disguise
the good book became a comic
read by fools with hollow eyes

they speak of making progress
while laying the land to waste
no wonder the fruits of their labour
contrive to leave a bloody bitter taste

questions stack unanswered
as greed stalks the corridors of power
and time mourns its lost days
stolen so slowly hour by hour

Two Sides

There are two sides to every story,
Said the boss to his staff
Pay you higher wages,
Are you having a laugh?
My profits keep us going,
And I invest what I can,
It works through paying low wages
To each woman and every man

There are two sides to every story,
But it's always the boss's side we hear,
Rarely is there a mention
Of exploited workers living in fear
My profits keeps us going,
And I invest what I can,
It works through paying low wages
to each woman and every man

Top Gear

Love watching Top Gear
Sat on the sofa with a pizza and beer
Laugh at the lads and their frolics
A reminder of playgrounds and exposed bollocks

Playing fast and breaking all the rules
Sniggering and giggling like uncontrollable fools
All good clean fun, or so we thought,
Till some beat upon snitch got us caught

Still can't say 'joy stick' without a stupid grin
Or forget the first pale faced girl I took for a spin
This is our culture, our visual wet dream,
Top Gear is class, far from extreme

Comrade

I'm not ashamed to call you comrade
Though many cringe and sneer
Claiming it's outdated, last century,
And perhaps slightly insincere.

Comradeship is what defines us
Links in an unbreakable chain
It's a bond forged through laughter,
Struggle and not without a little pain.

I'm not ashamed to call you comrade,
Stand by you when others doubt
I can't remain silent forever
Being united is what it's all about.

Disability Charities

Like to be charitable I really, really would –
There's nothing to say about disability charities
That would be positive or good.

They have a history of patronage,
Oppression and abuse
There's nothing to say about disability charities
Except they're no fucking use.

Let's be totally frank
Disability charities sell us short,
Because they're back stabbing greedy bastards
Who are easily bought

Like to be charitable
To Scope, Mencap,
Mind and many, many more
Help give them what they deserve
Take them by their throats then wipe the floor

They have a history of patronage,
Oppression and abuse
Their CEOs ought to represent old
Guy sat high
Upon the bonfire as we light the fuse

LOVE'S KEEPSAKE

Joe Cocker (1944–2014)

It just feels so wrong
That the man of steel has gone
But let's celebrate how long
We were entertained by his song

Poem for Liz

Someone has pressed your buttons
Left you more than slightly remote
There's a cry of utter frustration
Building up in your throat
Trying hard not to make
A complete spectacle of yourself
You throw your toys from the pram
And land them on the shelf
With a curse you seek control
But like silent witnesses they remain
Unmoved by your channelled anger
At having to watch a repeat again

Waiting

I'm not asleep
And I should be
Given up on counting sheep
Risking making future cups of pee
Money down the drain I can ill afford

Mind racing better than Lewis
Won't stop and that's the pits
In a tight corner
God, how I hate Tory shits
Flushed with success
Waiting for Greeks
Gift wrapped?
I can ill afford

White Rabbit

I feel we're being stripped of our humanity
And I feel it deep, down deep in my soul
As I observe the carnival of reaction
Chase the White Rabbit down a hole
I cling onto love like a raft on an angry sea
With sharks circling, waiting to upset me,
Wanting their pound of blood-soaked flesh;
Desiring to strip us of our humanity

But love is in danger when overtaken
By all the material things found in life
You want to own everything, care for none,
As you cause nothing but trouble and strife
I don't need a cold November day
To remember imperialism's brutality
As I watch the uniforms of hate parade
Their hypocritical homage to fallen humanity
I want to cling onto love like a raft on an angry sea
Feel the waves of emotion cascade over me
I want to see the White Rabbit emerge from
Underground and refuse to hide or betray liberty
I want to be part of 'we' not a chess piece
Strategically placed on a board like a pawn
This isn't some game of Kings and Queens
Or countless Mad Hatters yet to be born

We're talking not about the 'Land of the Free'
But the imprisonment of people from all walks of life
Who are slowly being stripped of our humanity
By those who cause nothing but trouble and strife
This is the punch of iron first in velvet glove
The agony of the last throw of the dice
We can't just lie down and take it,
And allow Earth to make the ultimate sacrifice

We must unite the green, red and gold
Use our tears to follow an everlasting rainbow
It's time for White Rabbit, you and me
To ensure hate fades and love will grow

Sense of Power

Drained empty by emotion
Stunned into silence by disbelief
I sit motionless and afraid
Feeling like a victim of a thief

Turmoil and confusion rain down
On my once dry secure parade
Guilt and love will drown me
As I sit motionless and afraid

Then as hour after hour
Passes relentlessly with ease
A sense of loss approaches
And suddenly I begin to freeze

I have a sense of power
Within this moment of negativity
It's the unknowing that's as painful
As the touch of my vulnerability

I'm drained and vulnerable
Making me powerless to intervene
Sometimes the sense of power
Feels so cold, bold and obscene

Power exists in between the lines
A controlling force we can't see
Convention dictates the surge
Of power that has silenced me.

Disquiet

It's completely out the bag
Sleep escapes me again
As disquiet echoes within
The silence of the night

Just Another Scrounger

I am just a name and number
scrawled across a case file
I am just another digit
within meaningless statistics
designed to engage,
employed to plant fear,
used to exploit

I am just a problem,
another lazy fucker
not biting at the bit
to oil the capitalist machine
I am just a face
among the crowd
you easily dismiss on a daily basis

Ms Whiplash

Ms Whiplash has a glint in her eye
As she, with her hand on her thigh,
Takes control of the situation.
With power firmly in her hand
She'll make him understand.

She seeks pleasure in his pain,
Cracks a joke at his expense –
And if he should carelessly bleat
She'll quickly delete
And he'll say no more.

Ms Whiplash dresses in plastic,
Looks quite fantastic,
As she invites him in
Again and again
To the Job Centre in town.

Disability Pride

I am a disabled person
not differently able,
physically challenged,
disabled.

I am a disabled person
not drenched with special needs,

or just the same as you,
different.

I am a disabled person
not a butterfly trapped
in a crippled body,
denied.

I am a disabled person
not willing to beg or roll over,
I am what I am
determined.

I am a disabled person
not ashamed to be a Crip,
but proud to piss on your
dogma.

I am a disabled person,
not a person with a disability,
so go play with your
definitions.

I am a disabled person
not part of your normality,
conned by your charity,
defiant.

Know Our Place

You should never get cross
Time to curb your anger
Stay mute in the corner
Out of sight and mind

How easy it is to boss
To judge and point a finger
Call everyone to order
And cull us from humankind

Cathy Can't

Cathy can't go home
There is no house or flat to rent
Since the cost of living went through
The roof and the benefit cap
Began this woman's hell descent

Material Failure

Heard the door behind me close
Where I'm going God only knows
And if he's spilling the beans
It's by some other means
Than through an email or phone call

Not into Karma or talk of destiny
All that stuff does nothing for me.
I'm into acting upon each concrete task
Identified, so if anybody wants a list, ask
That's all.

SENTIMENTS AND MEMORIES TO TREASURE

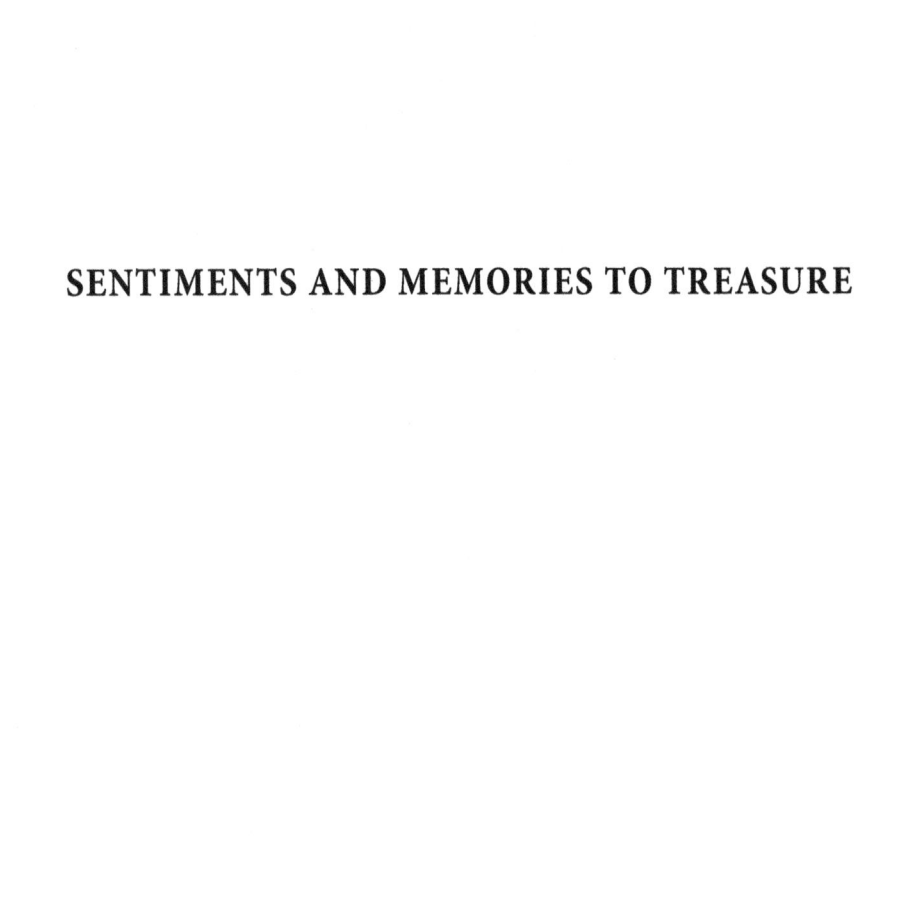

Love's Keepsake

I have given you laughter
With cheeky looks and clever words
To enhance your smile

I have given you my hand
To hold when troubles
Leave you unsteady

I have given you my promise
To be there for you
Each step

I have given you fresh hope
Instead of harsh criticism
And ridicule

I have given you comfort
When the cruel world
Took its toll

I have given you friendship
A bond that's strong
Between us

I have given you a chance
To believe in yourself
Once again

I have given you my love
It's yours to treasure
To keep safe

I have given you memories
Of our time together
Love's keepsake

Days of Sleepless Nights

Wide awake and thinking
Of my world that's shrinking
Contained neatly on the face of a postage stamp
My tomorrow waits outside in the cold and damp
Stood at the crossroads shaking
For my heart it's breaking
At the prospect of leaving in the wrong direction
Being fooled by the gaze of my own sordid reflection
Days of sleepless nights
Haunted by the talk of rights
Truth takes the embodiment of grains of pure sand
Then slips through my fingers becoming hard to understand

Wide awake and thinking
Of my love that's sinking
Down to where mermaids hide their ageless beauty
Free from the pressures of a cruel societal duty
Within a sea of possibility
They wait silently
Knowing it's the world above that's the real fantasy
Bound by painful emotions that won't set you free
Unreal and cold to touch
It doesn't add up to much
They spy me standing alone on the sandy shore
Worn out from all the thinking done the night before

Lovelorn

I'm lovelorn
Because I've been put out to grass
I'm tongue tied
Through having my words twisted
I'm all adrift
Knowing we're not all in the same boat
I'm falling
For the oldest trick in the book

You'll Need to Ask Yourself Why

When your heart is beating fast
And your mouth is as dry
As the most arid of deserts
You'll need to ask yourself why

When you can't sleep at night
And old movies make you cry
For no logical reason at all
You'll need to ask yourself why

Could you really be in love
Or is your mind just playing tricks?
Have you simply lost the plot
Or is this something you can't fix?

When your life feels it's on hold
And your painted smile's a lie
If you don't know where you're at
You'll need to ask yourself why

When you can't see the wood
Because the trees block the sky
There's only one course open
You'll need to ask yourself why

When I Tell You

When I tell you
I love you
It's not out of habit
Or to make polite conversation
I tell you I love you
Because you're the best thing
That's ever happened
To me

Mourning Memories Passing

hands of a clock with symbolic gestures
distance themselves from what was
as night chases day in an endless ritual

what was, now is, and soon no more
will be judged as a form of unforgiving,
merciless, cold-hearted progression

as with decaying leaves memories
with quickened ease attempt to escape
all the hurt that bitterly surrounds them

like some amateur thief in the night
who by clutching at straws seeks
to hold onto histories already stolen

Menu

Sunday morning
Emerging from
Clattering unwashed
Dishes
Her shapely figure,
Silhouetted by
Bright
Spat sunlight,
Caught him
Unaware

Words
Like undervalued
Exploited
Migrant workers
Slave away with
Little satisfaction or
Reward
As he makes a meal
Of the waitress
Temptress

I'll Never Lose You

Even if you were trapped in a bustling crowd
You ought to know that I'd cry out loud
Till we could reunite
I'll find you on the moving train
Even when the skies are heavy with rain
I'll search the darkness into light

I'll never lose you

The speechless bond is too tight
From early morning to late at night
It's in everything we say and do
If you are lost and can't be found
I'd doggedly behave like a bloodhound
Till I find my way back to you

I'll never lose you
Could you really be in love
Or is your mind just playing tricks?
Have you simply lost the plot
Or is this something you can't fix?

Forbidden Fruits

It's the longing
The knowing
The denial
That cuts right to the chase
It's the wanting
The questioning
The pumping
That quickens the heart
It's the dilemma
The lack of stamina
The fear of who we are
That plucks us from ourselves
It's the sweet taste
The taking in haste
The possibility of waste
That keeps all hope barely alive

A Miracle or Two

Wish I could replace the sun
That's fallen from your sky
Had an answer to all questions
That began with asking why

Wish I could turn the clock back
Prevent the pain you're going through
If only I had the power to
Do a miracle or two

You thought I could walk on water
Then turn that water into wine
You're familiar with these stories
But none of them are mine

I'm just made of flesh and blood,
Human, through and through,
I have no magic wand I can
Take out and wave for you

Wish I could right every wrong
That history tells with ease
And lift all the downtrodden
From their aching knees

Wish I could turn the clock back
Prevent the pain you're going through
If only I had the power to
Do a miracle or two

The only power that I possess
Comes from the beating inside my chest
That fires the desire to commit to
Doing what I know is best:

Stop wishing for impossible miracles
Look instead for solutions here on Earth
Have faith in the future of humanity
Rather than a child from a virgin birth

I Don't Get

I don't get to sleep at night
The devil's got my heart and he's holding on
Replaying the scenes from my life
Where the sugar-coated dreams are cut by a knife
And left dangling by a thread
I don't get to choose my day
The devil's pointed finger directs me on my way
To some distant horizon
Where the future plays out before the night has gone
And silence fills my head
I don't get to sing along
To the songs of freedom once sung one by one
By voices of those who dream
And tell stories of a world cruel and quite obscene –
A world that's not right
I don't get to sleep at night
I have a wolf howling endlessly in the moonlight
 Reminding me of who I am
In a world that's increasingly lost and doesn't give a damn
Or appears willing to fight

Duo

Looking for a second half
Someone to take my words seriously
Bring them alive and make them dance
Yes, it may sound daft
But sometimes poetry is incomplete

Without a musical refrain
So I'm still waiting a chance
To put together our song
But you've never offered to play
Along with my words

You Know I'm Into You

There are certain things I can't deny
And no matter how hard I try
Keep coming back to the same conclusion –
I have a problem: and you're the solution

You know I'm into you,
Yes, you know it's true, I'm into you

Call it madness, say I'm insane
Keep coming back to it, again and again,
Can't deny it because I know it's true,
I just want to make love with you

LOVE'S KEEPSAKE

You know I'm into you,
Yes, you know it's true, I'm into you

There are certain things I can't explain
But going on inside my brain
I've a powerful story of love and sweet romance
Where two people come together by chance

You know I'm into you,
Yes, you know it's true, I'm into you

This isn't about pure lust or plain desire
Although there's passion, a raging fire
What we have is love like a burning volcano
Will it erupt? Hell girl, I really don't know

You know I'm into you,
Yes, you know it's true, I'm into you

Want to take you way deep into my arms
Slowly unwrap all of your charms
Make your body sway like the waves in the sea
And keep you warm and safe for eternity

You know I'm into you,
Yes, you know it's true, I'm into you

When

When did I fall in love with you?
Was there really a time and place?
Because there hasn't been a time where
Your beauty has failed to hold my gaze
Or made my heart flutter like wings

When did I realise you'd stolen my heart?
Was there really a time and place?
Each time you enter a room my heart
Leaps from my chest to greet you
And when you leave the absence lingers

When did I become spellbound by your smile?
Was there really a time and place?
If your smile were the sun, my heart fresh snow,
I know it would melt every time your lips
Send their magical warmth in my direction

When did I need you more than I do now?
Was there really a time and place?
My life would be incomplete without you,
Each day you give me purpose, hope,
And most of all; provide a reason to believe.

When did I fall in love with you?
Was there really a time and place?
My love can know no boundaries
Nothing can contain the power that lies within
But it's yours for as long as we are one

Promised Land

In the quiet of the night
For a fleeting moment
I caught sight of the Promised Land
Tasted milk and honey
And lived the dream
I'd held in my heart

In the quiet of the night
Hands wandered across
Both cold and warm terrains
Seeking moist satisfaction
Amongst the hills and valleys
That lay in wait

In the quiet of the night
I trembled at the sight of such inviting
Beauty that stretched beyond
My comprehension to engulf desire
Drowning me in overwhelming passion
Within the turmoil of a desert storm

In the quiet of the night
With lips, fingertips and tongues
We loved and were loved
Knowing each movement
Could be the last chance
To glance at the Promise Land

Pause for Thought

In the silence I wait
Hoping for a connection
Through human interaction
But the silence keeps on going
Sending me a message
Loud and clear:
There's no point waiting
The connection has been
Broken

When We

When we talk
Our words run away
Like droplets of water
On a parched tongue
Refreshing, energising,
Freely expressing

When we laugh
The magic of fairies
Is caught in our eyes
And the sound that's held
Upon our lips
Echoes with a sweet refrain

When we are
Who will see what's there
Beyond the silent knowing,
Disapproving looks
That stand in judgement
But without the right to condemn

When we love
No words are needed
The magic has engulfed us
The sentence can't hurt us

If You Want to Hear Good News

Take tomorrow by storm
Leave no stone unturned
Open up your heart
Raise the roof
Stand together
And seize the time

If I were

If I were a duvet
I'd let you wrap yourself inside me
If I were a bank
I'd let you let you take the credit
If I were a freezer
I'd let you chill for a while

If I were an open book
I'd let you read between the lines
If I were a writer and poet
I'd let you have chapter and verse
If I were words
I'd let you sentence me

If I were completely lost at sea
I'd let you come and find me
If I were certain
I'd let you know for sure
If I were brave enough
I'd let you see me cry

Fishing

He went fishing for crumbs of comfort
But she wouldn't let him off the hook
He tried hard to spin her a line
But she still refused to take the bait

Spades

You don't need to lie
To bury the truth
Ambiguity, distraction, omission
Act as good spades

The More You Deny It

The more you deny it
The more I think you want to try it
Your steadfast refusal
Is just your attempt to bamboozle
You say I'm to blame
But I think you feel just the same

I'm standing on the edge of time
Searching for reason without rhyme
I know if I take a step I'll drop
But your silence says, don't stop
Yes, I know I'm a complete fool
It's the heart that wants to rule

All the things floating in my head
They're all best left unsaid
Please tell me that this is no joke
See my life going up in smoke
Come on, give me a clue,
Even better, tell me what to do

I know what I feel isn't fake
But my heart fears it'll break
If it goes all out on a limb
The chances of success are slim
But the more I think it wants to try
The more I need to deny

I'm Thinking

I'm thinking I should be doing;
Doing things I should've thought about;
About to think this wasn't such a good idea
A good idea doesn't come from nowhere;
Nowhere is where I am because I'm thinking

If I Could…Would I?

If I could wake from this dream
Be free from the silent scream
That tastes bitter-sweet
And then put time into retreat
Would I?

If I could find the point of no return
Prevent the last bridge from starting to burn
Know how to unlearn
Walk straight and never turn
Would I?

If I could be in denial
Perhaps only for a little while
Could I change the way I feel?
Help the wounds I have heal
Would I?

If I could be strong and walk away
Never to listen to anything you say
Pretend I never felt the way I do
Find the courage to lie to you
Would I?

Thief

One minute I had it beating inside my chest
But then she stole a kiss from me
Now there's a silence beneath my vest
And I'm feeling all at sea

Like a thief in the night she came along
Got her two hands upon my heart
Then it dawned on me; it had gone
Replaced by the memory of a kiss

Missing You

Even before the door closes
I've a sense of loss
And I feel incomplete
That's why I'm missing you

Even before your scent
Leaves the air around me
I know I want it to linger
Until you come back again

I'm not me without you
Just a shadow of who I am
You make me smile so much
That's why I'm missing you.

Thinking Once Again About What Might Have Been

Wanted you by my side
When we went for a ride
But I had to admit defeat
When a couple nicked the seat

Had to gaze from across the aisle
Shoot you a pleasant smile
Behaved as a gentleman should
Preferred to have snuggled if I could

Wanted to feel your warmth by me
Every inch of our long homeward journey
But that couple put pay to my secret hope
So I guess I'll just have to cope

Thinking once again about what might have been

I Promised

I promised to let sleeping dogs lie
And allow boats to remain quite still
Pretend that what we know
Never happened, never will

I promised to keep on walking
And never be tempted to return
Never let you cross my mind
Or go and make your ears burn

But each promise I make
Just means I live another lie
There's a different truth
And I need to know why

A promise needs to be forever
But the writing's on the wall
I wasn't trying to be clever
And spill that old apple cart

I promise to be who I am
To face the mistakes I've made
Not to deny what love is
But to call a spade, a spade

Love Poem

"How do I grab you?" I said,
feeling for an opening,

"Two handed," she replied.

I Would

If I could live within your smile
Bury myself in your laugh for a while
Linger forever on your tender lips
Feel you here from head to finger-tips
I would

If I could occupy your heart
Or even a tiny little part
My own would leap so high
A thousand tears I know I'd cry
I would

If I could hold your beautiful gaze
Love you in so many different ways

Travel to all those distant lands
That you outline in your plans
I would

If I could make dreams real
Let you know just how I feel
Have hold of your trembling hand
And help you to understand
I would

U r

U r the jigsaw's missing piece
The 1 called in 2 keep the peace

U r my sunshine on a rainy day
The 1 who likes 2 laugh & play

U r the verse making the poem complete
The 1 who never fails to turn up the heat

U r a constant when others leave
The 1 able to help me to believe

Distance

The Distance
Between
Our smiles
Equals
The distance
Between
Friends
And
Lovers

Between

Between
You and I
Lies
Nothing
Nothing
But sweat

Caught

Caught between
A rock
And a hard
Place
Means
I can't
Make a move
On you

What You Are

You are my book-mark
The question-mark at the end of the sentence
My light within the darkness
The spark that lights my fire
The chord that strikes within my sleepy heart
The pain in my arse that won't let me be

Agenda

Slowly, softly, she entered into my world
And before I knew it
Nothing was as it once was.
Dreams were no longer far fetched
Rights were back on the
Agenda

ANCIENT AND MODERN

Against the Odds

Disability can be a lonely
And painful experience
Nevertheless with love and solidarity
I believe we can succeed
Even when the odds stand
Long or are
Stacked against us

Bridges Start to Burn

Somewhere along life's journey
I must've taken a wrong turn
For in my rear-view mirror
I see bridges start to burn

There's no way back now
I must take the road ahead
But do I follow my heart
Or the voices in my head?

I look out for signposts
But they're few and far between
And nearly all of them seem
To point back to where I've been

But in my rear-view mirror
I see bridges start to burn
Guess I'd better just keep going

As I've nowhere else to turn

Maybe I'll get lucky
And find a hiker along the way
One that understands my journey
And will be prepared to stay

Shaun the Sheep

Every time I try to sleep
All I ever hear is the bleat
Of Shaun the sheep
He's stuck in my head
Between the covers of my bed
He's quite obscene
That creature made from plasticine

Why?

Why use a thousand words
When there's only three I need?
Why would I cut off my right arm
And sit and watch it bleed?

There are many questions in my head
As many as there are stars in the sky
Trying to explain how it is
Just leaves me asking, why?

I've found a road to travel
Although I don't know the journey's end
Will I ever reach my destiny
If I'm not accompanied by my friend?

Friends are what help to make us
The people that we become
So if we lose the one who really matters
We end up more than a little lonesome

A friend is someone to trust
A person you can rely on too
So, my friend, I hope this explains
Why 'I love you'

Our Name: It Is Invisible

Their shame, embarrassment, disappointment
Dress us up as invisible and ensures we are
Out of sight and free from their minds
As creatures time forgot we have no place
Among those who already mourn our passing,
Regret we ever were in the first place
Our bodies condemn us to being viewed as
Crimes against humanity, deserving of
Merciful deaths and set free from imprisonment
It doesn't matter who we were or who we are today,
Or which hand struck to remove us from
Their shame, embarrassment, disappointment

LOVE'S KEEPSAKE

Little Step Back

Can't see the wood for the trees
Bitten off more than you can chew
Find yourself in way too deep
Take a little step back

If the weight of the world is crushing
Thousands of fingers pointing at you
Remember, there are only four cheeks to turn
Take a little step back

No sense in playing the martyr
No benefit in acting like a fool
Pick your battles, my darling
Take a little step back

My love is waiting
To shelter you from the storm
Don't forget I'm right behind you
Just take a little step back

The Beauty

The beauty of the ambiguity of Mona Lisa's smile
Is captured on your lips
A smile that holds so many inviting secrets
On lips which remain knowingly silent

The beauty of the jet-black universe where stars
Have fled in order to appear in your eyes
Lies above and below the surface
Of my gaze as I struggle to take you in

The beauty of the moment stored in stolen
Memories rekindle your smile
Returns the sparkle to your starlight eyes
And gives you hope for eternity

Rain

When there's a single rain drop
No one really notices or cares
But if the rain comes down in sheets
Then everyone stares
We are being soaked by emotions
And drowned by grief
The outpourings are endless
Which means there's little relief

No Doubt

I'm looking for excuses
Reasons to question
The slightest of doubt
As fear stalks me

I'm looking for answers
To questions I daren't ask
I've become a fallen angel
And of that, there's no doubt

No doubt I'm to blame
For the ache in your heart
The longing that you feel
Because of a man like me

I turned your head around
With words that spoke
The language you understood
And needed to hear all along

Do I need to plead for mercy
Ask you to try and forgive
For I've burdened you with my love
And of that, there's no doubt

Ever

Ever felt Judas' kiss?
The touch you couldn't resist
As the flames of naked desire
Grew higher and higher

Ever lost touch with your soul
Scored a massive own goal
As you watched life fall apart
With the shattering of your heart

Ever blinked away tears
Twinned with memories of years
Where you suffered in vain
As he betrayed again and again

Ever reached out for the door
Knowing that beyond there's more
Than you'll have if you stay
But you see guilt standing in the way

Ever felt Judas' kiss?
Betrayed by the life you miss
Shattered heartfelt dreams appear
Reminding you that you're still here

Intoxicated

Is my glass half empty
Or about to over-flow;
Will I ever find out?
Do I really want to know?

You have a full body
And I long to drink you in
Would you call me besotted?
Would that be such a sin?

I can taste you on my lips
As perfect as any wine
Can you tell I'm intoxicated?
Will you ever be mine?

Land Of Make Believe

Perhaps we're away with the fairies
In the land of make believe
But I'd rather live on the edge of possibility
Than be utterly sad and have to grieve

I'm going to take my chances, darling,
If and when they come along
Can't rely on fate or fortune
Just need to be where I belong

Perhaps we're away with the fairies
Counting clouds one to nine
But I'd rather live on borrowed time than
Lose out on what could be mine

I'm going to take my chances, darling,
If and when I can get to roll the dice
I want to dream so I can make believe
Go somewhere I don't need to think twice

I'm going to take my chances, darling,
And wear my heart on my sleeve
Going far, far away with the fairies
To live in a land of make believe

No Chance

Think I want to say goodbye
Turn my back on all we've been through
Nothing ever stays the same, I know
But give me one good reason to go
That's not what I want to do
Wouldn't even try
No chance

LOVE'S KEEPSAKE

You Are

You are my first to last
Concern each day
A permanent feature that
Never goes away
As constant as the heart
Beat in my chest
The reason why I
Find it hard to rest

You are the centre of
My personal universe
Where there is no rhyme
Or reason to curse
The love I never knew
Until you took hold
And gave me
Shelter from the cold

You are the impossible
Dream come true
The desire that burns
Forever for you
The reason to believe
Beyond all doubt
You are my jailer who
Will never let me out

Melt

three in the afternoon;
with life ebbing
from me
in the sweltering heat
of the classroom,
I see the invitation
from her
'come to bed eyes'
and melt

No One Breaks My Heart, Like Me

Some people say they can read me like an open book
Others claim they need far more than a second look
Many times I've heard it said that I'm hard to believe
When I say I can wear my heart on my sleeve

I know it's true that I don't suffer fools gladly
Or tolerate bullies going around acting badly
But my bark is often seen fiercer than my bite
As I'm more interested in getting things right

There's a silent river that runs ever so deep
Hurting when witnessing others start to weep
Raging with anger at the sight of inequality
Truth is no one breaks my heart like me

LOVE'S KEEPSAKE

I judge myself by standards that are hard to maintain
So I experience a constant war going on in my brain
People tell me to slow down and try to get some rest
But I'm always thinking and putting myself to the test

No one knows better than a revolutionary like me
The personal price of fighting for others' liberty
Loved ones are left to look on with total disbelief
As you sob with bitter tears at a stranger's grief

While there's injustice, poverty, and pain
Come sunshine or come sheets of rain
I'll take a stand and refuse to leave
Because I can wear my heart on my sleeve

Single mother in Stoke or child in Baghdad
Their plight can make me feel really sad
I can't turn away and pretend I don't see
Truth is no one breaks my heart, like me

We're on the Same Page

We could just talk for hours
About the weather or some theory
There's never an awkward pause,
Sharing a laugh; why it's easy

We're on the same page
Know where we're coming from
Like two peas in a pod
We've a friendship that's strong

Take tonight, what did we do?
Told me you were feeling down
So I put away my serious face
And became your personal clown

That's what friendship means;
Being prepared to go that extra mile
Listening to all that's said
Trying to bring out a special smile

We're on the same page
Know where we're coming from
Like two peas in a pod
We've a friendship that's strong

We're the best of friends
Keeping each other together
When theories are out the window

And we're facing stormy weather
Take tonight, what did we do?
We laughed till we cried
Closed the door on a cruel world
So we both had peace inside

We're on the same page
Know where we're coming from
Like two peas in a pod
We've a friendship that's strong

What Am I to You?

Please tell me what I am to you?
Just another man standing in queue
Someone on your fanciable list
Or a lover you can't resist

Turn me on, you know you do,
Shoot me a smile right on cue
Have my heart on a piece of string
But does any of this mean anything?

What am I to you?
Will you ever show, let me know,
What I am to you
Will you have me and then let go?

LOVE'S KEEPSAKE

People say you like to tease
Get your men down on their knees
Have them crying out for more
Just before you shut the door

Please tell me what I am to you?
Do you feel the way I do
What's going on in your head
Am I just another notch on your bed?

What am I to you?
Will you ever show, let me know,
What I am to you
Will you have me and then let go?

Turn me on, you know you do

Ought to know what I am to you
And I know you love me too
There are people out there ready to hurt
Brand you nothing but a flirt

Know what they're saying is wrong
What we have is something strong
Shouldn't let words cause me to doubt
Because we both know what we're about

LOVE'S KEEPSAKE

Empty Shore

It's not the fading sound
Of her dying breath
That leaves me stranded
Upon an empty shore

It's just the painful ease
With which I stay
Grabbing some last moment
I should've had before

    Oh don't you cry for me
    For I won't cry for you;
    I touched your life
    With the palm of my hand –
    Now all I can see
    Are colours changing
    Through the falling sun
    And the forever shifting sand

Inside your smile now
Our love remembers
Where apples lie decaying
Without Adam Eve regrets

Taking your hand in mine
Maybe not an act of love
But far more than just\
A few last personal effects

    Oh don't you cry for me
    For I won't cry for you;

LOVE'S KEEPSAKE

I kiss the pictured lips
So still and so sad;
Brush against the fallen hair
Lying, waiting for me

Turning my face to the wind
I catch the coldness in my eye
No longer can I hear
Breaking waves of a deathly sea

Endless Day

When night fails
        to leave
its calling card
and the business of the day,
with all its stress and strain,
        feels so hard
think of me

  When the touch
  of sunlight falls
  gently on your face
and the softness
        of the breeze
gives you a sheltering place
        think of me

  When the shimmering grains
of whitened sand

are licked upon the shore
and the sea
of blue
returns home once more
think of me

When distant thoughts
no longer have a hold
or seem too far away;
and life is but
a glimpse
caught timeless on
an endless day

When will you think of me?

Dipping my Toe in the Water

Hesitated, holding my breath,
Unsure of what to expect,
The unknown depth
Would it overwhelm me?

Tentatively, eyes distracted,
Compulsion starts to take over
Temperature slowly rising
Edging closer to the moment

A slither of light casting shadows
Captures the threatened stillness
Dipping my toe in the water
Wait of expectation finally over

Brighton

The days were roasting
And the nights were warm
On our way down we were coasting
Despite the distraction of searing heat

Urgently needed a change of scene
Planned our secret getaway
Never told anyone where we've been
Kept our photos on private view

It was a moment never to forget
Relaxed as we soared into the sky
Those days I'll never regret
I've photos and memories on private view

Welcome to Britain

Welcome to Britain
We'd like to invite you in,
But, first, one question:
What colour is your skin?

Because if you're Black,
We might send you back.
If you're a Pole;
Will you try to claim Dole?

Welcome to Britain
What languages can you speak?
If you don't fit into our culture,
Could be gone within a week.

Because if you're White,
You might be all right,
But if you don't sound like a Brit,
Might treat you like shit.

Welcome to Britain
With our imperialist past
We're scared shitless
The empire will strike back at last.

Too Painful

    The hands on the clock
                      Stand upright
    Calling me to attention
                      It's the hour I dread
    Despite being filtered
    The news is too painful
                      Cuts deep like shards
    Of ragged glass
                      Broken in pieces
    No different to my heart

I Just Want to Love You

I'm just lying here looking at the ceiling
Wondering why I've got this feeling
I'm losing control of my senses
Letting down all of my defences
It feels so good, but it isn't right,
I just want to love you tonight

Just lying here pretending it's not real
Because I can't deal with how I feel
There's something going on for sure
My heart's signed a declaration of war
It feels so good, but it isn't right,
I just want to love you tonight

I'm just lying here, if I deny how it is
Must find a way to get through this
Can't explain what's going on
How can happiness be wrong
It feels so good, but it isn't right,
I just want to love you tonight
I'm just lying here looking at the ceiling
Wondering why I've got this feeling
My heart's signed a declaration of war
Yes, there's something going on for sure
It feels so good, but it isn't right,
I just want to love you, alright?

Once

Once upon a lifetime
Something quite out of the ordinary
Disrupts the mundane
Sends shivers down the spine
Quickens the heart
Changing everything forever
For better or worse
Perhaps only time will tell
But for the moment
She remains silent

There Are Things

There are things that can be said without words
Such as with the look within sparkling eyes
You can know you're loved by a single kiss
Or a pounding heart that's hard to disguise
There are things that can make perfect sense
Without there being either rhyme or reason
You can know the warmth of love's touch
During the bleak days of the winter season
There are things that can defy convention
Give us hope despite all the odds
Refuse to accept the cruelness of defeat
By putting fate in the hands of the gods
There are things that can keep you going
Even when everything is falling apart
Sometimes there's no rhyme or reason
To explain the beauty of a pounding heart

Lost in Thought

Thinking too deeply means
Being lost in thought
Like a blanket thrown over signposts
Memories cover the direction
I came from but offer no clues
As to where I might be tonight
I know I need you darling
But you're independent and strong

Can't expect you to travel with me
Even though we get along
Lost in thought

We don't live within conventions
Much to other people's distain
Find it hard to play by the rules
That are often lost in thought
And way too hard to comprehend
Together we are trouble
To those who get in the way
For I'm thinking a change is coming
As I sit and watch you thinking
Deeply lost in thought

When You Are With Me

Sometimes I can see my reflection
And fail to recognise the man I've become
Can't say I gain any satisfaction
For many of us growing old isn't fun

Aches and pains of daily routines
Are sure reminders of years gone by
My memory still clings onto scenes
Although at times I really wonder why

When you are with me
We can turn back the hands of time
Back to when we were young and free
And the days were forever yours and mine

Books stand on guard demanding attention
Pictures hang from each and every wall
A mirror curtly tries to dismiss my reflection
As yesterday's dreams lurk untidily in the hall

Is this the person I've finally become
A shadow of the man that I used to be
For many of us growing old isn't fun
Not like the days when we were young and free

When you are with me
We can turn back the hands of time
Back to when we were young and free
And the days were forever yours and mine

Waves

Want to make waves with you
Do what I can to rock the boat
Jump right in at the deep end
Hope you'll keep me afloat

Dear Life

Dear life
From the moment I was forced from my mother's womb
You've made me struggle each step of the way
Perhaps the balance I've never had
Can be found in the words I've written instead
Today, I feel my heart has been locked in a tomb
And you are refusing my plea to stay
As the goodness in the world turns bad
The sadness is taking its toil inside my head

Dear life
How can the past hang so heavily around my neck
It feels like one of those yokes oxen might wear
I can hardly move under your weight
Not knowing what you want or expect from me
Today, I feel my heart is being held in check
Too fragile to listen to the words you want it to hear
You really think you can hold my fate
When all around me is saying I'm lost at sea?

Dear life
The journey has had so many twists and turns
Along with all the various ups and downs
Love has both come and gone again
Such is life I suppose you might say
Today, I feel my heart is cold rather than burns
Its passion has been stolen by an array of clowns
In its place there is nothing but ache and pain
But life, I know tomorrow is just another day

The Scales Weigh Heavy

The scales weigh heavy
In one direction
Rather than with balance and harmony

Without peace there is no justice
Without justice there can be no peace
Without love the scales will remain heavy
In one direction

Caught up in Someone's Dreams

Said we were so close
From across a deep divide
But I always sensed I was missing
Something deep down inside

Said there was a need
Wanted me to pleasure without pain
But when it came to loving
Never offered me the same

Now I'm asking
If what I see, is all that it seems
Am I just fooling myself
Caught up in someone's dreams

Said that all that glitters
Can't be viewed as gold
Sensed there was a fire raging
Although the embers were cold

Said we were so close
But was there something to hide
I really tried to love you
From across a deep divide

Now I'm asking
If what I see, is all that it seems,
Or am I just fooling myself;
Caught up in someone's dreams

Proximity

We occupy the stage
Although we're worlds apart
You have the power
But I have the desire
Which of us is closer to winning?

Tea and Sympathy

She wanted to give me
Tea and sympathy
Make me her good cause
For the day
But all I desired
Was a mug of coffee,
A slice of Dundee cake,
To send me on my way

She offered me a prayer
To save my lost soul,
And to send her
No doubt, Heaven bound
Yet all I could say,
As I dug a big hole,
Is: 'Life might not be fair,
But my politics are sound'

She cursed me
Way beyond damnation,
Said I wasn't worthy of
Her tea or kind act of charity,
As I stood to leave,
There was a slight hesitation,
I cleared my throat with a cough
And said, 'Piss on Pity'

You and I

You are the thirst I can never quench
You are the bolt I can never wrench
You are the reason I can never rhyme
You are the guilty I can never fine

I am like the well that has been drunk dry
I am like the tear that refuses to cry
I am like the question that you never ask
I am like the player that is taken to task

Like an Eagle That's Taken Wing

Like an eagle that's taken wing
He spies his prey far below
Sitting pretty, unaware, oblivious
Of the silent predator circling

Talons stretch with anticipation
As he swoops down to make
His kill, seize his prize, fly away
With the wind beneath his wings

In an instant she is up,
Twisting, back and forth, in
And out of the shadows
Frantically seeking an escape

Did he strike, claw his way
To success or was her speed
Far too quick for him; leaving
Him snatching at thin air?

When he awoke the poolside
Had cleared, a strong wind
Blew across the balcony, and
The bikini-clad beauty had fled

Within the Silence

Within the silence
Nothing stirs
Everything hangs
In hibernation
Small creatures
Sleep
Oblivious to the world
Around them
Lost
Within the silence

LOVE'S KEEPSAKE

You're Wondering

You're wondering what I'm thinking
As I stand here without blinking
Truth is, I'm past caring
Done with all that sharing
Sick of watching you creeping
Hoping our people remain sleeping
Never been for unity
Using your power against me
Regarding me as a rival
A threat to your survival
You try to undermine my integrity
Destroy our solidarity
You can set your hounds free
Plotting to rip to shreds democracy
But it'll all be in vain
Knock me down, I'll just rise again
You may burn and rip
But I'll never abandon ship

Outside our Comfort Zone

We talk as we journey
Along the asphalt surface
Seeking to avoid potholes
In both path and argument
Trees sway
Even if neither of us bend
Ripples on the lake
Spread out from the centre
Perhaps in an attempt to
Communicate
We are completing the circuit
Outside our comfort zone
Trying not to get stuck
In our ways

Critical Acclaim – Offer a Little Light

It's not that I dislike your style
Or think your material isn't good,
It's just that, once in a while,
Try to offer a little light if you could

You capture the world of pain
From every angle there could be
But I don't really think you realise
How depressing that sounds to me

LOVE'S KEEPSAKE

Your audience all applaud you
The press give you critical acclaim;
So why change a winning formula
 What would there be to gain?

I don't want to undermine you,
Belittle what you've managed to achieve
But sometimes uncritical voices
Can only help to deceive

Sure you capture the world of pain –
A journey many have travelled before –
But if you only offer shades of grey,
Then the only exit is a trapdoor

It's not that I dislike your style
Or that your material isn't good,
I just fear that all your intentions
Could easily be misunderstood

You say you want to entertain
But you don't offer a little light
You only sing of a world of pain
So there's no hope in sight

I don't want to undermine you,
Belittle what you've manage to achieve
But sometimes uncritical voices
Can only help to deceive

SOMETHING OLD, SOMETHING NEW

Life

Life has many twists and turns
Sometimes we miss the plot
Feel the pain as hopelessness burns
End up gambling with what we've got

In life there's no repeat or pause
Life doesn't take a break for a while
We live it the best we can because
Death can't make us smile

I'll love you come what may
If that makes me a fool or a clown
It'll be for others to judge not me
But I'll never let you down

Life has to be lived, love given
Not a simple dress rehearsal
It's not all romance, tied with ribbon
Life can be harsh day after day

For the Canny, Nothing New

They observed from a distance
As the fanfares and parades
Announced his ability to walk on water
Slay the dragons and the monsters
Hiding behind his rhetoric

Their silence turned to disquiet
When the dragons spat fire and monsters rose
And beyond the surface when all had sunk
The hopeful and exposed were left to pick up the pieces
For the canny, of course, it was nothing new

Nothing Obvious

Perhaps I'm in a trance
More than just standing there
Goggle-eyed and laughing
At nothing obvious

Some might call it romance
Being caught up in a togetherness
No one could ever have predicted
Or sought to define

And so tonight we dance
Souls feeling intertwined by the passion
And the music pulsating through
Our sweat-covered bodies

It's too late to sit on the fence
We have embraced our futures
And cast doubts to the wind
As the romance leaves us laughing

Drift Away

I should close my eyes
And let the troubles of the world
Drift away
Into the space vacated
Allow dreams to come calling

I should close my eyes
So I can picture you in my world
And drift away
In between the space vacated
By the touch of your calling

I should close my eyes
Dream of a shared beautiful world
Where we can drift away
From the vast space vacated
Into the sea of love that's calling

Habit

There is a moment just before
We say our good-byes and part
When I begin to feel a sense of loss
A sharp pain in my heart

Probably I should be familiar now
With the tide of emotion that flows

But the truth is, I hated it,
Each and every time she goes

I'm not in the habit of speaking
In a language that's simple and plain
But here goes, I'll try and explain
The cause of my continued pain

Do you know what it's like to see
Your own reflection, hear your views
Voiced by another who shares
Your feelings about the news?

Do you know what it's like to laugh
At the jokes that only you two can share
Or poke fun at things you've done
But still have time to care

Do you know what it's like to miss
A piece of the jigsaw you need to fit?
To realise friends are a bridge to happiness;
And being together is much more than just a habit

Looking Sheepish

That guilty look lined his face
It was no longer possible to disguise
He had become a national disgrace
For pulling the wool over people's eyes

When Dreams Come True

When dreams come true
And happiness floods in like
Sunshine on a bright summer's day
Seize it with both hands

When dreams come true
Smile inwardly and feel the glow
Fill your heart and soul
With utter contentment

When dreams come true
Life becomes a little more bearable
Bonds strengthen with certainty
And tomorrow doesn't hold as much fear

When dreams come true
Know they were meant to be
Be not afraid to dream
And live in expectation

Body Fascism

Plastic cards for extra bits and bobs
Let's all join the ranks of the fashion snobs
Vanity's but another form of stupidity
What the hell's 'human nature' or normality?

Don't want to wear a suit and tie
Wear designer crap – I'd rather die
Body fascism makes me a freak –
Dress the beautiful, scorn the weak

Sell the body as a commodity
Turn the ordinary into an oddity
Beauty becomes a form of plastic
Body fascism sees me as a spastic

Edge

I'm standing on the edge of time
Questioning what's really mine
People make such a fuss
About things that fade to dust

How can you ever be free
If you don't own your insecurity?
Live your life like an immortal god
Before disappearing beneath a sod

Here we stand upon this fragile earth
Not really appreciating what it's worth
We can all talk about love and romance
But how many get a second chance?

I'm standing on the edge of hope
The future swung tied to a rope

Now I'll stretch out my empty hand
To grasp what we fail to understand

If time was really on our side
Our insecurities we wouldn't hide
But neither tide nor time waits for us
As all things fade to dust

Mermaid

You were my mermaid
Always there to make waves
Swim against the tide
Far from being
A mythical creature

Train

Too many thoughts
crammed like
a commuter train
inside my skull

Insecurity patrols
my wakened hours
keeping sleep
at a distance

Temptation stalks
my conscious brain
like clockwork in
an unforgiving manner

Solutions stay
hidden from view
inside a crammed
commuter train

No Recollection

I'm looking back as history escapes my gaze
What was, is now clouded in a haze
Names and faces begin to blend
So I can't spot a beginning or an end

The candles are burning out as the light fades
Memories come and go like figures behind shades
Sands of time are shifting all too fast
Soon I'll have no recollection of the past

Expectations

An expectation is a belief that is centred on the future and may or may not be realistic

Carry my expectations to the extreme
So disappointment comes like showers in spring
Confusing dreams and expectations
Can end up with a familiar hollow ring

Expectations can change in the test of time
Realism can blow as harsh as a desert storm
Carving out holes without reason or rhyme
Leaving expectations battered and torn

Maybe I should lower my sights
Stop setting the bar way too high
Put an end to all those sleepless nights
Where I lay awake asking why

Why is so much out of our control?
Why isn't it possible just to
Let the good times role
Accept you can only do what you can do?

Maybe it's true, I expect too much,
Want my dreams to turn into reality;
Maybe my expectations are out of touch
In the hands of a man like me.

That Time After Midnight

Sometimes the day just passed
Only leaves scars instead of traces of memories
Reminders of things begging to be forgotten
You must have come across
That time after midnight

Never Know

Never know which way to turn
All roads lead to despair
Bridges continue to burn
The doubters are everywhere

You'll never know unless you try
But you refuse to understand
And I can't see why
You bury your head in the sand

Complain that the risk's too high
Then quote from the Sun or Daily Mail
Never mention those who'll die
Or what will happen if we fail

You tell us it's a foregone conclusion
And the writing's on the wall
But is this just spin and collusion
With stories that are more than tall?

We'll never know if we don't fight
Put up some form of resistance to it all
Time to rise and seize the time
United we stand, divided we fall.

Perhaps

Perhaps it was the step too far
The possibility that knew
There was no way it could be realised
Outside the wild dreams and fantasies
Of a man frantically grasping at straws

Perhaps it was the hope fading
No different to grains of sand
Slipping out of control through fingers
Unable to prevent the inevitable
Fate of someone frantically grasping

Current Times Are Shocking

Sometimes, I must confess, I do detest
So many of those among the rest
Who sit upon their arses
Complaining about the upper classes
Yet pick on the so called vulnerable and weak
But then next minute kiss their other cheek
What planet are they on?

One where love of humanity has gone
A planet where you worship The Sun
And shout screw my neighbour and everyone
What planet are we from
One that rewards people for doing wrong

Leaves old, sick and disabled people to their fate
Encouraging self-hate on the council estate
Sometimes, I must confess, it's too much to take
I lose the will to live as my heart starts to break
People have bought into the "me, me, me"
Forgetting about the planet and equality

There's racism and homophobia on the prowl
But people are more interested in Simon Cowell,
Too busy trying to make ends meet
To be bothered about the lady down the street
How do we stand firm and turn the tide
Stop the sheep from being taken for a ride?

Current times are more than a little shocking
Overhead the vultures are busy flocking
We need a revolution; we need to plan
Time to make the rich carry the can
Make them accountable for causing the decay
As witnessed by the ice melting away

LOVE'S KEEPSAKE

I Can't Find Myself

I can't find myself
In the words you speak
For I'm absent from your thoughts
Till some charity
Shakes a tin
Under your nose
But how do you view me then
As you relieve yourself of
Your money
Your guilt
Your responsibility?
Perhaps as
An object of charity
Devoid of any humanity?
I can't find myself
In the words you speak
You don't speak my language
And as a result
You refuse
To understand
Me

There are still words

There are still words
Unsaid
Floating inside my head
Unable
To escape from the sentence
Unfairly
Passed over in a moment of thought
Unlikely
As that possibility might sound

After the Storm

Like a wreck,
caught upon a seashore –
She lies
battered,
brittle,
perhaps a little broken by time
Promises of youth,
smashed thoughtlessly –
Anguish now
lurks within
stiffened limbs
Once, where beauty stood –
now traces of betrayal
leaves witness
to the past

An index finger
points cautiously
at the lover
never considered
never wanted
Here lies woman,
condemned by circumstances
beyond reason
Like a wreck,
caught upon the seashore –
Innocent victim
of
Man's cruel
world

Bosnia: Holocaust II

Buildings lie crumpled
Resembling tossed away
Crisp packets
Strewn carelessly
As death stalks like
A wounded beast
Seeking unsuspecting victims
Of circumstance
Innocence flees as the advance
Of cruelty gathers momentum
Threatening to engulf like
A raging fire

Children deep cry with hunger
Mesmerised by the fear
That grips as tight as
The hand of the long lost mother
It's the dress rehearsal to your
Final solution
It's the unfolding drama that
They promised never to repeat
But as the directors and producers
From the United Nations argue
Over details
The Holocaust arrives for another
Audition

Mirror Girl

> i'd hate to
> see
> the back
> of
> you

Taken

You see them on TV
Talking hysterically about destruction
With such sweet seduction
It makes you want to come
To believe some
Of what they're offering you
Come on, admit it's true

Painting pictures black and white
Colourless dreams to fright
And the bogeyman under your bed
Was planted in your head
As you were taken in, so it's said
By the clown at the BBC

Speaking so hysterically
Better dead than Red
Prefer a trip to Switzerland instead?
They let Laura spin and spin
A web to entice you in
And you'll be taken by the hand
To see a corporate brand
Stretched across the land

Don't cry out or weep
As you have nightmares of sheep
Marching your way to save the day
Turn off the TV, listen to me,
Don't believe all you hear and see
And avoid acting hysterically

LOVE'S KEEPSAKE

The Keeper of My Heart

Gave you my love in a heartbeat
A repayment for the beauty
That shone through everything
You did and freely shared

Love Still Endures

The page may have turned
Credits begun to roll
Sunset upon the horizon
Love still endures
Harsh words cut like a knife
Candles struggle to flicker
A desert storm rages on
But love still endures

Desperation line faces
Hunger gnaws deep within
As hope hangs by a thread
Love still endures

When everything feels nothing
Touched by the cold hand of fate
Despite all this and much besides
Love still endures
Love still endures
Love still endures

Memories Caught

Frozen in time
I struggle to be free
No different
To the fly in the web

What is
Is not what was
Revisionism can't
Eradicate the scars
Or substitute for forgiveness

You Turn Away

I approach you with a smile
Hoping you'll come out to play
But you have other plans
And without a word you turn away

I stand wondering why you
Had nothing to say to me
Is there something I should know?
Your behaviour is a mystery

Perhaps I expect too much
After all, Rome wasn't built in a day,
But how can we create anything
When challenged, you turn away

You're quick with your negativity
Always willing to knock
Rarely do you offer a solution
Or have a key with which to unlock

Your behaviour is a mystery
The negativity turns my feet to clay
Is there any point in trying
If all I do is make you turn away?

Off Guard

Didn't see it coming
Wrapped in a lyric, photo, memory
It threw me and landed a punch
Grief is unpredictable, raw
Caught me off guard
When my defences were down

LOVE'S KEEPSAKE

Never Mind

Never mind what it says on the label
It's the fucking tin
Without an opener
That does your head in
But the real drama is under the table
Where all the crumbs collect
Just that little bit out of sight
So it means you don't reflect
On the things that truly disable
Creating a world full of shite

Never mind what actually took place
All that matters is being a poet
Set free to roam a council estate
But nothing's real, don't I know it,
The lies line right across the writer's face
Caught on camera in a still
Like an image paused in a TV drama
And when you've had your fill
You're caught out by karma
As it bites you on the arse

Never mind the anachronistic tone
From another place or time
Let music be today's fast food
And who cares if it fails to chime
You're inhuman if you seek to moan
Dancing on Ice provides granny's fix

Safely in her incontinence pad
Already fed and watered
Reliving the life she once had
Praying to Jesus on the crucifix

Remembering Little Big Horn

Surviving on the fumes
From an age the history books distort
And where films glorify the colonialists
While vilifying the unnoble savages
Who are we to condemn,
Biden and Trump happily concur,
As the pair of cowboy Presidents
Ride shotgun for a nation of thieves
A nation of hypocrites
Who pontificate about God's word
While engaging in decades of evil acts
That merit being turned into stone

Past Tense

There are words on the paper
Although they make little sense
Why, I ask myself, is so much
Narrated in the past tense?

The last thing I wanted to do
Was leave the bridge far behind
Yet the truth is that the flow
Of life can appear quite unkind

We are players caught on stage
Forbidden the right to rehearse
Each day brings its own challenges
Revealing the pleasure and the curse

As age brings forth its own decay
Time is a reminder of the past
No matter what we might believe
Nothing is really ever built to last

The Magpie

I see you gather bits and pieces
From God knows where
Placing them inside an ivory tower
You've built over there

The plan is to have a nest egg
Paid for by the empress's new clothes
Sold at extortionate prices
To eager sycophants treading on toes

Your heady mix of eclectic materials
Bamboozle the all too willing
Thirsting after everything like rabid dogs
The sight is more than a little chilling

What you serve up is intoxicating
But leaving behind a bitter taste
Although this goes unnoticed
Among those who drink in haste

The magpie rhyme is said to predict the future
But in its ivory tower
The magpie predicts nothing will come other than
Babbling sycophants to be fooled by the hour

First Time

From the first time
You entered my world
Nothing was ever the same again
Tried to hide it
Even sought to deny it
But everything was in vain
The first time I saw you
My heart was lost

The Family

Here, look, look,
Shoot, shoot, shoot,
See the mother
Surrounded by her children
They were captured
Framed

This is no photoshop
No manipulation of the scene
It is there in black and white
Apart from the blood
They took the shot
But it wasn't with
A camara

Maybe

Maybe I should've trod a different road
One that was to lead to a pot of gold
Instead I followed my heart
Even though I knew from the start
Only sunshine and showers, my friend,
Never to find a rainbow at the end

Maybe if I could've seen my destiny
The man you clearly wanted me to be
Wouldn't be in a different time and space

Etching sadness across your face
But it's easier to know after the event
Where all the hopes and dreams went

Maybe the old hands of time could turn
Back to the days where passion would burn
Hope was eternal and dreams inspired
Those were the days before I retired
No longer able to talk the talk
Let alone attempt to walk the walk

Hear is the News

Listening to the news
Reminds me of naughty children
Who have something to hide
And rely on lies to cover their tracks
Propaganda trips off the tongue
With such ease it becomes naturalised,
Guilt is a softer touch than Andrex
Better too at defending the indefensible
There's a race to see which stacks up
The quickest and highest;
The body count or war crimes,
Either way, the West doesn't give a fuck!

Use Your Mobile

Use your mobile will soon be
The final words of many
Who decide to screw with me
You see, I fume
When I hear these words
Used by arseholes who assume
Everyone has one
Use your mobile is an instruction
That renders the brain, heart,
Or any other body part
Facing possible future extinction
Your mobile will soon control
Everything you need to do
It's best spade for digging the hole
Everyone has one

So Many People

So many people
Want to keep it simple,
Straight forward, uncomplicated,
Packaged in black and white
Without ambiguity, without doubt,
But that's Alice in Wonderland
At some Mad Hatter's tea party.

So many people
Aren't interested in politics
Too busy cussing immigrants,
Spying on the benefits cheats,
Talking about Gary Barlow's next million
Choosing the right home
For their old mum and dad

So many people
Stick to their safe routines
Sitting watching TV all night long
Switching over when the news comes on
Rather watch a Dad's Army repeat
Than have to hear again about some
Bloody war going on God knows where
So many people
Just want to have a quiet life,
Free from pestering protesters,
On about things that don't concern them
Such as global warming, poverty,
The arms trade, whatever that is,
And, of course, wrong VAR decisions

So many people
Happy to believe what Boris said,
Doubt the moon landing and the pandemic,
Thanks to something seen on X
And the same people think the Russians,
Or did they say the Chinese,
Produce ninety eight percent of all fake news

Miss You

So tired of listening to my own voice
But guess I'm left with little choice
God knows, I paid the ultimate sacrifice
See, I've never been good at taking advice

We both were completely headstrong
Neither prepared to admit to being wrong
Trading punches in an exhausting fashion
Delivering blows with untold passion

Then when the volcano was about to blow
Each of us in our own way would know
It was in that moment we'd realise
The only way forward was compromise

Now my thoughts have nowhere to go
Absence of challenges or an instructive no
Find myself living in a state of incomplete
The drive I once had has learnt to retreat

Too much time and empty spaces
Painful memories of familiar places
So hard to find things to do
When my chief occupation is to miss you

Making Sense of Contradictions

So many memories seep into the present.
Each step of the journey I feel you there
Then again, in an instance, sense absence.
Things at first sight look the same as once was
But on closer inspection will never be.
Questions go unanswered, advice unheard,
Nothing feels as lonely as contradictions.

Display

They turned gaslighting into an art form
Crafted from guilt and remorse
Hung on newsroom walls
Their sculptured reality placed on display

Each form twists the truth into a knife
Begging belief to commit self-harm
Plunged deep into the now sceptical heart
Truth becomes the willing killer

The oppressors are the corpses
Mothers of terrorists aged three or four
The victims are the artists
Who display in the Gallery of Lies

LOVE, LIFE, AND LONELINESS

It's in the Moment

When reality catches you off guard
Mimicking the strong wind taking your breath away
You can't anticipate or build defences

Reality always discovers a way
To leave you flat footed, completely unaware of its approach
It's in the moment

The cold hand of fate shakes you
Bringing your vulnerability to the fore
Stripping you naked and alone

Nothing can prepare you, protect you, reality and fate combine to rock
The foundations that appeared so stable
Before you found yourself in that moment

Secrets

They are what is not known
Or seen or not meant to be known
Or seen by others

I have secrets which weigh heavy
Sometimes I feel I am bound
To drown in untold awareness

LOVE'S KEEPSAKE

They are safe, hidden away,
Although I am not a safe, just
A keeper of knowledge best unknown

Secrets that could tell of pain
Or of love suspected, but never confirmed
Or things that could easily destroy

Atlas carried secrets, not a god
He travelled with secrets
That threatened to make him fall

Sleepless nights are the price
Paid for suffering in silence,
For protecting others' guilty pleasures

As keeper of knowledge best unknown
There are lessons that ought to be learnt
But the wisdom sought lies in shadows

Shadows prevent us from seeing
Allow innocence to stay unfettered
Relying on light to bring into play

My hands are tied, bound by reasons
I am unable to acknowledge
In the fear of what might be revealed

Secrets weigh heavy, dragging me down,
Drowning me in things I would rather
Not know or have to pretend do not exist

Treading Water

Was that yesterday or the day before?
One of those days, there was an interruption,
A friendly face at the front door.
She smiled, widely, trying hard to hide an assumption
About the look that she might have seen.
But I quickly adjusted the mask, before she asked,
A patronising question, I'd find obscene.

Becoming quite an expert at treading water
Letting everything just float above my head
Highs include bowel movements, seeing my daughter,
Being thankful the phone doesn't ring instead
Or Messenger late at night doesn't give a fright
Through some form of miscommunication, an illusion,
That gets right inside your over anxious head.

How it was, is certainly not, the way it appears
Days and nights merge into weeks flying
Memories struggle to recount all the years
Punctuated by too many old friends dying
Age, they say, is really just a number
Counting up or counting down, you decide.
Treading water, an awakened slumber.

Between a Rock and a Hard Place

There's nothing to compare with that feeling
Caused by the vice-like grip of guilt
As it places you without mercy or compassion
Somewhere between a rock and a hard place

No different to a fly foolishly caught in a web
You struggle until you are exhausted
Unable to move, trapped, destined to remain
Somewhere between a rock and a hard place

Completely paralysed, you have no choice
Other than come to terms with the guilt;
Accepting actions have consequences for those
Somewhere between a rock and a hard place

Minute to Minute

It's like kicking through autumn leaves
They fly high in all directions
No longer settling where they once were
Disturbed and waiting to be caught
Unawares at any time

This is my minute-to-minute existence
Flying in all directions and no longer
Able to settle down and live as if
Nothing is going on, nothing has been left

Behind in disturbing memories

That uncertainty hanging like a threat
Paralysed by the fear of doing, saying
All the wrong things you know you
Could have said and done before the milk
Turned sour once split

Contradicting myself as I toss and turn
I promise not to repeat my mistakes
But accepting there's every chance
The well-worn path will welcome
Me home as it has many times

The colours of the leaves dance
Within the chill of
autumn madness
Where everything begins to decay
In anticipation of a barren winter
Of endless nights and frozen days

Looking for Answers

The owl on the branch
Claimed his name was Sherlock
And his wisdom was far from elementary
The words gave him a chance
But then decided to take stock
Because he kept dithering over an entry

LOVE'S KEEPSAKE

Looks as if the Die's Already Been Cast

No point trying to explain, it's a pain,
Heard it all before, I'm sure.
So, where to start, I opened up my heart,
The reason I'm feeling bad, took all I had.

Want to know what's wrong, well she's gone,
Heard it all before, went out the door,
Yeah, it's a pain, she's not coming back again,
Lessons learnt, always easy to get burnt.

They said these feelings wouldn't last,
So much for catching on fast,
How can I care for tomorrow, still living in the past?
Looks as if the die's already been cast.

Some things are hard to forget, still I regret,
The words I said, now they're stuck in my head,
My mistake seen at a glance, no second chance,
Well she's gone, that's what's wrong.

There's a look on my face, and an empty space,
Where my heart once lay, but she took it away,
It's a look of disbelief, how am I still in grief?
Answers escape me, need to let it be.

They said these feelings wouldn't last,
So much for catching on fast,
How can I care for tomorrow, still living in the past?
Looks as if the die's already been cast.

Ghosts from the Past

Ghosts from the past conspire
To visit havoc on the present
Rubbing salt into the historic scars
Made by mistaken actions
And the echoes of guilty pleasures

Man Made

As humanity self-destructs
The planet sees seas rise
Tears for those who worship
False gods man made

The greed and hypocrisy
Fills the air as everything
Chokes on the products
That man made

On the surface scars exist
Due to boundaries carved
From the thirst for power
Nations man made

Humanity's inhumanity
Sowing and reaping
Recycled paths of despair
Too often man made

Carelessness abounding
Plants, animals, children,
Like lambs to the slaughter
Upon alters man made

As temperatures soar
Reflecting the embarrassment
Nature feels for the world
Man made

Rising Tide

Is King Cnut their role model?
Commanding nature to obey,
While acting oblivious
To the heat waves coming their way

If You Were to be Believed

If you were to be believed:
There are no tyrants craving power
Ordering bodies to mount by the hour
Never have we ever seen politicians lying
Or witnessed innocent children dying

If you were to be believed:
Then truth is something quite absurd
It is right to hang onto newsreaders' every word

The sky always appears to be white at night
As bombs rain down; is that not right?

If you were to be believed:
Some omnipresent being grants free will
To go and steal, rape, and, of course, kill
While sat on His everlasting misogynistic arse
As everything neatly comes to pass

If you were to be believed:
Humans are nothing more than docile sheep
For what they sow is what they reap
The iron fist in a velvet glove
Is the Church's way of spreading love

If you were to be believed:
We should simply fall into line
And accept capitalism is divine
That democracy is safe in politicians' hands;
Hands that clap ethnic cleansing in other lands

Praxis

Imagine an idea, no different to a stone;
You might hold it, turn and feel its surface,
Reflect upon what you have in the palm of your hand,
Before putting it to some practical use,
And then evaluate how useful the stone has become

Reflecting upon yesterday

The flow of the river takes us down stream.

As part of its journey, it becomes an artistic director: transforming and reshaping the landscape.

It leaves behind what was, while seeking to imagine and nticipate, what might be.

We cannot change the past, but we can reflect upon yesterday, re-evaluating or re-interpreting what it might mean to us today or tomorrow.

The course of the river, an endless transformation, has a beginning and an end, but between, each movement alters what was, is, and will be.

Like a river we meander upon our journey, gathering material to shape the future. Yesterday has gone but within reflections caught as memories it will become like the river, an artistic director, providing a means towards the end.

LOVE'S KEEPSAKE

The Words on the Page Were Like a Knife to the Heart

I wanted to be in denial, even just for a while,
Making sense of your passing, where do I start?

You were the wordsmith supreme and your peers all say so.

Sharp, witty, rolling with the punches, you were the way to go.

Despite being a Villain, you could do no wrong.

Your words conjured up magic, always powerful and strong,
You couldn't be bought, be subjected to assimilation.

Original, breathtaking: I can admit you were an inspiration.

It's Like the Itch You Can Never Reach

It's like the itch you can never reach
The unsolved mystery that keeps you awake
Lessons that are too difficult to teach
The heart only you had the ability to break

Just when the ground feels secure
Something comes along knocking you off your feet
Love never plays by the rules, that's for sure
Each step you take is bitter sweet

Not knowing is the worst kind of torture

Because it slowly eats away bit by bit
There are times when you can picture
The everlasting fire burning in hell's pit

I'm judged as a sinner and doer of great wrongs
Found me guilty without producing proof
Relying on pointing fingers and wagging tongues
Had no qualms about ignoring the truth

Why did you choose to be judge and jury
Punishing me for failing to live up your expectations?
Was it the outcome of scorn and fury
That finally fed your deliberations?

From Tiergartenstrasse to Treloar

Different times
Different places
Nevertheless both crimes
National disgraces

If you fail to see
How the two relate
Better go study your history
Before it's all-too late

Where Do You Begin?

It's not that I've nothing to say
It's just the words get in the way
Yes, I need to simply confess
Feelings I'm unable to express
Every sentence becomes a lifetime
Handed down with no reason or rhyme

Too much water has flown by
It's far too late to question why?
Why there's no words able to explain
The depth of this forever lasting pain
Guess here's the thing
Where do you begin

Sean

Sean, this is the day you were born,
We still mourn your passing,
But your legacy will be forever lasting.

You were stubborn as a mule
Unprepared to be anyone's fool,
Be silenced, fobbed off, used as a tool

Took up the fight for independent living
As for Tories, you weren't forgiving,
For freedom and justice, you were driven

When Time Stood Frozen to the Spot

When time stood frozen to the spot
The hands on the clocks covered their faces
With no past to reflect upon and no future
To encourage dreams or secret desires
Meaning packed a bag and quietly left.

With clocks falling silent as a consequence
Of no longer having time on their hands
Day and night purposely went on strike
Refusing outright to allow the candle
To proceed to burn at both ends.

Frozen in time and without meaning
Nothing mattered, therefore, questions
Joined a militant day and night standing
On the picket line as the candle
Sought out a place to openly sulk.

Why had time become so fearful
That it could no longer move with ease?
Was it jealous that nothing appeared
To have secured undeserved attention
Thus forcing questions to be redundant?

Without questions there was no point
In having answers, so they followed
Meaning out of the door in search
Of a purpose if such a thing could exist
Now that nothing really mattered.

Knowledge

Without the thirst for knowledge
The unaware sip slowly
From the fountain of ignorance

True Colours

Directly behind the battered keyboard
The man sits with fingers at the ready
His eyes, razor sharp, patrolling the scene
Too many culprits to put to the sword

He will strike when good and ready
Questioning his truth is quite obscene
There is a glint of deep satisfaction
As he watches the snowflakes fall

The protector of the like minded
Acts without a moment of hesitation
Always there to answer the call
Of the offended and blinded

The take-down is swift and sweet
Dismissing the bleat of free speech
He slashes right to the chase
A good slap puts them into retreat

Silencing the liberals who preach
Watching the Reds leave in haste
Nothing produces a sense of fury
More than those who stay and fight

But he will go toe to toe for hours
To justify being both judge and jury
Longer the battle, the greater insight
His victims have of his true colours

Intimidation

Who would have thought
Some find my thoughts,
Words, and actions,
As threatening as those
Of the Kray Twins?

What Might Have Been

Watching the sands of time
Tumbling from top to bottom of the hourglass
Reminds me of how easily opportunity can slip away
One minute it is there full of possibility
And the next it becomes a reflection of what might have been
Time and sand between fingers
Fall as we fail to control the moment due to hesitation,
Fear of failing, and lack of faith in our own ability
To embrace the moment and go with the flow
Enjoy what is rather than focus on what might happen

I Am Not

    I am not a Time Lord,
    Able to go back and change the past,
    Unfeeling what I felt or remove the scars
    Left behind as a consequence.

    I am not a circus performer,
    Able to juggle with emotions and clown around
    With painted tears streaming from my eyes
    And lips than even outdo Dolly Parton's.

    I am not a dogmatic fool,
    Able only to listen to my own counsel,
    To totally believe my own thinking
    Without reflection or critical appraisal.

I am not a wise man.
Able to protect my heart before its broken,
Avoid opening old wounds or sidestep pain,
I am a fragile human, with time to reflect.

The Love Affair

The small TV sat on the bedroom's floor
With a reception that struggled to exist
I was watching 'Top of the Pops' because
There was nothing better to do.
Suddenly, towards its conclusion, I saw
You appear as a new entry into the charts.

Never imagined that moment would also mark
Your lasting entry into my heart.
The list of singers, groups, and genres, I love
Is too long to capture here, but you always
Take pride of place along with Carole King,
Simon and Garfunkel, Bob Marley and The Clash.
Forty six years on, the Greatest Flame,
Still burns as strong as every hill, river and road
That takes me home to you, my country, culture,
The high road to Scotland where I belong.

Alternate Reality

It's not that we're on a different page,
We're not even in the same book!

Why should I deny a constructed lie?

Perhaps if I tried to take a look
At where the sun doesn't shine
I might catch sight of your reality
Which certainly isn't mine.

Aftermath

The in-between, quiet acceptance of negation,
Lost in signs of disapproval, all framed indifference.
Void of explanation, wild thoughts saturate
The space left behind with unquestionable ease.

No trial, only the sentence, stretching endlessly
Into the darkness and terrifying fear of what might be
Lurking buried in the unconscious mind filled with
Guilty thoughts which are left to their own devices.

The paralysis of indifference takes hold,
Unmoved by appeals for forgiveness from the heart
Already shattered and left bleeding by the wayside,
Discarded, yet still trapped in yesterday's dreams.

Kafka and Poe add clarity within the aftermath
As nightmarish images crowd around
Substitute jury members left unemployed
In a world made uncomfortably cold by indifference.

Discourse

We dance around issues,
Like a woman with a handbag,
With everyone demanding to have their say.
After hours of debate, clarity fades, spirits finally sag
The bulldozing males relentless till they have their way.

Austerity

Neoliberals of every hue
Cut corners so we go
Around in ever decreasing
Circles

They point their fingers
At the cleaners, the poor,
Anyone blocking increasing
Profits

Banks accounts are dry
As greedy bastards demand
Fur coats to cover their naked
Lies

Cotton was hand picked
By the Union Jack draped knight
To be the eunuch standing
Guard

We pay the price for neoliberals
Disappearing to where
The waning sun struggles to
Shine

2023

If I'd seen you coming, I would've hidden,
Words that describe you perfectly well
Are completely forbidden
On Facebook and in polite circles.
How to evaluate the highs and lows?
I can't be objective, you were a nightmare,
God only knows
From the personal to the political, you stank.

Nothing to Fear

Out of the mist, suddenly, it was clear
Without a doubt, nothing to fear,
Behind smoking mirrors silhouettes
Dance away those sad regrets

Took the bait, suddenly, caught,
Situation looked on, rather fraught,
No exit appeared within the spotlight,
Surrounded by dishonesty, bound tight

Time is an imitating river in full stream
It carries everything as if in a dream
What once was, is now as good as gone,
Distant memories of what went wrong

Without a doubt, nothing to fear,
The nightmare is no longer here,
Spell broken, scars instead of hooks,
Beware of beautiful covers on books

Self-respect

Society constructs walls to keep us in and out
But the bars upon our prison doors are fashioned by self-doubt
We internalise embarrassed silences and turned away looks
Forever grateful for patronising praise when writing books
We crave their approval but fail to equate it to the pat on the head
We passively accept their gushing at everything we've said
Even when guilty of talking or writing utter shite
Some on Facebook will still state that it sounds all right
Our pride and dignity we'll never successfully protect
Until the day we can set ourselves free by gaining self-respect

Lambs to Slaughter

They dangle as they hang onto every word
No matter how devoid of history or absurd
The fallen heroes of an age gone by
Have no voice and therefore have no reply
The sheep happily graze in ignorance
So willing to be lulled into a trance
By the hypnotic sound of your party line
Recycled, repackaged, but in decline
In forever decreasing circles you spin
Like a spider and its web, luring them in
Trapped, but in reality a gullible prey,
Taken in by what you had to say
When truth becomes the sacrificial lamb
Minds close tighter than a clam
Politics turn into nothing more than a farce
While sheep are put out to grass

Partners in Crime

Don't compare us to Bonnie and Clyde
Our crime wasn't robbery
We fought against the law
That failed to give justice and equality

Together we stole a march
On those who talked the talk
But when push came to shove
They could neither wheel nor walk

LOVE'S KEEPSAKE

As partners in crime we rode into battle
Fearlessly taking stride for stride
We had each other's backs
Fighting always, side by side

Images of Kati

turning dreams to reality
images of totality
embrace
without a trace

black and white
colours bright
flash and still
caught at will

Kati stands
moving hands
Kati lies
sparkling eyes

candlelight scenes
vegetation greens
laid bare
mustn't stare

radiant sun
with beauty spun

as shadows cast
from your past

Kati sighs
with knowing eyes
nothing's what it seems
reality turned to dreams

Satanic Verse

Thought things couldn't get any worse
But then realised there'd be all hell to pay
Said you saw yourself in the verse
The result being; you cursed me all day

The Same Old Story in a Different Disguise

You approached me with a smile,
Saying, why don't you stop awhile,
I'd like to know a thing or two…

My heart began to thump and race –
Sorry, I'm just a user in this place,
Besides, who the hell are you?

Can't believe my ears –
Can't believe my eyes –
It's the same old story,
Just a different disguise!

With a smile growing in size
You mentioned a consultation exercise –
Lucky me, straight out the hat…

We've reached question sixty four,
Don't think I can take much more –
Just another fifty? Fancy that!

Can't believe my ears –
Can't believe my eyes –
It's the same old story,
Just a different disguise!

Told you what I'd like to see
But were you listening to me
With your glazed over eyes

Now what would I do in your shoes
Tied in red tape and water tight rules –
Offer the same old story in a different disguise?

Passive Resistance

Sometimes
Silence can say more
Than a thousand
Words

Death can be
Induced by no more

Than a cursory
Glance

Time can be
As erosive
As the blast
Of a desert
Storm

Behind
Folded arms
And narrowed eyes
I wait

If Only

If only we had had the courage
To take risks and push
On the door that was partly
Ajar

If only we had been more
Adventurous and peered
Beyond the distant
Horizon

If only self-doubt had not
Held us back and allowed
Opportunities slip through
Fingers

LOVE'S KEEPSAKE

Children in Need: the Saville Row

Feeling all alone
In need of a good moan
But there's no one here

Had to stand my ground
Or risk being pushed around;
Nevertheless the weight of criticism still hangs in the air

Tried to make them see
My objection was the hypocrisy
That lies behind the lies at the BBC

They just wanted my child to conform
Accept and play by the norm
After all, they said, what's the harm?

How easy people are fooled
How easily they are ruled
Thinking there's a natural gulf between rich and poor

Jimmy Saville knew how to fix it
Hiding behind playing the latest hit
For years inflicting pain

They cut their cloth to suit
Power is always at the root
Of their manipulation

Of course, when they're able
They quickly turn the table
Make me the villain

Reckons I looked out for number one
Despite all I've said and done
Everything falls down on me

It made me feel wild
That they'd use my own child
To defend depraved charity

There are Things to Forget

There are days that bleed into an eternity
As seconds sluggishly haul themselves
Across the face of a clock that has seen
Too much action disguised as love.
There are memories that fade quicker
Than the sun tumbled from the sky
Guided by the screaming of those who
Witnessed every moment the first time.
There are futures unborn and at risk
Of never seeing the light of days to come
Because darkness is descending like
A shroud ready to cover the naked truth.
There are echoes of the here and now
Lying beyond our imagined comprehension
Rebounding back and forth no different
To a football endlessly kicked against a wall.

WORDS AND MEMORIES TOGETHER FOREVER

This is Albion

The sound echoes around
the near empty stadium.
Within an hour there will
be a rising tide of clamouring voices.

People sat like ants in the distance
wait in anticipation, tinged
with a measure of apprehension,
knowing what will be will be.

This is Albion where nothing
comes handed on a plate;
but does history always favour
the brave?

Socialism

'Socialism, if it's worthy of its name, means human relations without greed, friendship without envy and intrigue, love without base calculation.' – Leon Trotsky

Is this not worth every muscle strained,
Every minute given over,
Each alternative activity missed,
All the questions forced to answer,
The thousands of dreams on hold?

I Wish I Could be in Denial

I wish I could be in denial,
Convince myself it was a bad dream.
One I'll wake up from shortly
Then let out a sigh of relief.
Unfortunately, the truth,
Brighter than the sun high in the sky,
Helps cast a shadow long
Across this ill-considered ploy.
Like the catching of breath
Suddenly, out of nowhere, dawn
Brings home the realities
I long to pretend don't exist.
Foolish thoughts trade places
No different to children playing
Upon a merry-go-round
But without the fun of the fair.
Accepting what is, becomes
A painful tug-of-war, unforgiving,
As the truth battles with denial
In an endless struggle.

LOVE'S KEEPSAKE

Sophie Ann

Sophie Ann is a quiet recluse
A night creature rarely seen
She dresses for a camera and
Smiles for the mirror
Which promises to keep
Her secrets on reflection

Sophie Ann wears her dresses
Like a queen going to a ball
But there's no glass slipper
Only a mirror smiling
As she takes one last look
Before surrendering to the day

A day may come when she
Will feel the sun on her face
And proudly wear her identity
Unafraid of the whispers,
Sideways glances, and laughter,
That keeps her living in the shadows

My body

My body is trying to tell me something
I really can't quite comprehend
There's a discomfort in my chest;
Is my heart playing up, the beginning of the end?

I've had hypertension before
It's really far from nice;
But how do you explain a discomfort
To people without a good record of giving advice?

So I'm seeking answers to questions
I'm really struggling to formulate
Because the feelings I have are indescribable
And that's why I hesitate

Peter Tosh

He stands proud –
A lion on the prowl –
Dreadlocks hanging free
With a heart beating fast

Him a brother
In the family of life
Him a thinker
Who had vision
Him a star

LOVE'S KEEPSAKE

That lit our life
Him a rebel
With no fear of oppressors

He sang his songs
With the strength of armies
As he offered reason
To cool the fires of iniquity

Him the I
Burning in the living soul
Him the I
In every sweet kiss of freedom
Him the I
To unite those they divide
Him the I
Who sought to understand

He sharp as a razor –
Cut deep and long –
Through their meaningless
Ideologies and false morality

Him the singer
the poet
the revolutionary
the Rasta man

Thank you

Thank you for your steps and stairs
Thank you for your laughs and stares
Thank you for your aggravation
Thank you for your segregation

Thank you, thank you, thank you,
Thank you, till eternity!

Thank you for your special schools
Thank you for your benefit rules
Thank you for your ring-and-ride
Thank you for your day at the seaside

Thank you, thank you, thank you,
Thank you, till eternity!

Thank you for your medicalisation
Thank you for your patronisation
Thank you for your pathetic image of me
Thank you for your TV spun charity

Thank you, thank you, thank you,
Thank you, till eternity!

Seriously, of course, us Crips
We know that without your kindness
All those things would be behind us;
So, please forgive, our ingratitude

LOVE'S KEEPSAKE

And this might appear rude –
It's time to, cough, cough,
Thank you to simply and quickly;
Just fuck off!

Take No Prisoners

They walk the streets as if they own the place
Not a trace of an emotion flickering on the face
Of the man with the eyes behind the gun
Protecting the relics of a dying empire in the sun.

As beads of sweat dance and fall down his forehead
He recalls a life he left far behind for dead.
Where the nobodies stand looking bored to tears
Without enough money for the next round of beers.

> It's a case of take no prisoners
> You must learn to fight just to survive
> And if you fail to make the grade
> There's little point in staying alive.

He swapped the uniform worn on the terraces –
A general in an army of angels with dirty faces –
For the uniform worn by the professional elite
Who walk so tall and proud down the street.

Once he was condemned as a street-fighting man;
Was it Chelsea, Millwall, or maybe even West Ham?
Knives and fists that once flew for fun and pride
Now replaced by the machine gun resting at his side.

> It's a case of take no prisoners
> You must learn to fight just to survive
> And if you fail to make the grade

There's little point in staying alive.
Once his hate was based on the colours of a team
He now understands what being a patriot could mean
From Liverpool to Commie scum, from Celtic to IRA
Fighting for king and country was always his way!

He understood about colour and creed
Blacks and Catholics can both die and bleed.
His flag and country he'll gladly follow –
Belfast today, but where tomorrow?

Badge of Shame

They took the flower from the field
Where you lay bleeding, crying,
Dying as the consequences
Resulting from their greed.

They took the wire from which you
Crawled, battered, beaten, and
Twisted it around the bodies of
Young men in symbolic fashion.

In hospitals of rehabilitation, you
Are fashioned into tragic victims
And left to make poppies for
Pennies not pounds.

Do we recall on Remembrance Day,

'The land fit for Heroes',
'Lest we forget', or the thousands
Ignored and living in near poverty?

The poppy is a badge of shame,
Not a symbol of pride.
While you treat them as cripples
Their comrades needlessly died.

Rollercoaster

Being taken on a ride with twists and turns
Rising and falling with every promise made and broken
Inside my torment rips me apart as my frustration burns
When will I know I'm included and not just a token?

Like a cat, I can't keep still on a hot tin roof,
For I'm waiting for your call to give the green light,
But your silence makes me wonder if the truth
Is that everything is far from right.

Being kept on a rollercoaster against my will,
Being pushed and pulled all over the place
Is it little wonder I'm starting to feel
I'm going to be left with egg on my face

Circle of Love

You stand there like a child
Example of a repeated movie scene
You want me to comfort you
But all I do is act tough and really mean

> I know it's hurting you –
> That's what hurts me too!
> How can I explain?
> Here we go again…

You never speak your mind
But now you expect to communicate
You always remain mute
Try responding before it's all too late!

> I know it's hurting you –
> That's what hurts me too!
> How can I explain?
> Here we go again…

It's a circle of love, circle of love,
It has no beginning, has no end
Can't see the join
So why try to pretend?

You stare at my broken face
Example of a story long forgot;
You want me to comfort you
But how can I be something I'm not?

I know it's hurting you –
That's what hurts me too!
How can I explain?
Here we go again…

You wait for a little sign
To put the pieces back together again
You hope to discover a smile
And carefully ease all the hate and pain

Empathy

Your intellectual ability
Enables you
To identify with
Me

In all honesty
You have no idea
How gratifying that
Is!

Besides, I know
You are all too aware
It's impossible to put
Yourself in the shoes
Of the beggar

You can, nevertheless,
Have empathy
Express moral outrage
And I know I

Owe you
Without a doubt
Boundless amounts
Of gratitude

You see, once I had
Empathy with
A white, male,
Christian Social Democrat

It was easy because
I could intellectualise
Standing snugly inside
His shoes

Old Man

Old man,
I never knew you
But, how I miss you now
Words of wisdom
Fill my aching head
As I read your testimony
And the things you said.

Old man,
The Revolution lived
Inside your eyes
Only wish I could
See it now –
Hope fading
Somehow.

Old man,
Death took you from us
Because you knew too much
Tears fill my eyes
For those who now look
Up to you
Seem out of touch.

Old man,
They read your words,
Failing to understand
That in order to organise
A Party, first, you must
Invite The People

Revolution Betrayed

It was not a chess tournament
Played with kings and queens
Though pawns were in great supply
Rationale and logic portrayed a chequered history

Santiago 1973

'The City is the grave of revolutionaries' – Fidel Castro

The radio is bent
low over the bowl –
it is screaming
crazy words,
spewing out unwanted
truths in a depressing
moan

Somewhere
life lies
naked upon
a computer

Somewhere
the distorted
voice crackles
above the violent
bursts of interference
as thousands
weep

They are compiling
the news
in the blood
of the innocent

As the radio spews up
a head
of an
Eagle

LOVE'S KEEPSAKE

An Observation

You are the master
Of stating the obvious
The judge said, passing sentence

There's Nothing Unusual

Sometimes deep inside –
Words come so hard to speak.
Confusion comes to fill my head,
And its pain leaves me feeling weak.

The sadness comes from knowing
There's something hidden in my heart,
Sometimes I feel it overflowing,
Will it upset the apple cart?

Some things are best left unsaid
But how can you lie about loving?
Confusion comes to fill my head,
Wish I knew exactly what I'm doing.

For there's nothing unusual
In the ways I feel about you;
Don't need help from magazines
Don't need to go back to school

LOVE'S KEEPSAKE

All I need is a chance
To sit and think it through,
For there's nothing unusual
In the ways I feel about you

Somehow the thought of confessing
That I'm in love with you
Leaves me cold and sweating,
Not sure what you would do.

The fear comes from knowing
There's a secret deep inside my heart,
And once I let it out;
Why, I've upset the apple cart.

Some things are best left unsaid
But how can you lie about loving?
Confusion comes to fill my head,
Wish I knew exactly what I'm doing.

Empty Rooms and Meaningless Smiles

Night falls outside
And suddenly I'm alone
There's no sound of footsteps
No voice to be heard on the phone

Cups stained with coffee
Lie scattered across the floor –
Feeling a little sad –
Maybe even more than before

Now we have empty rooms
Without those meaningless smiles
Yet the distance between us
Can still be measured in miles

Life stands for nothing
If all the dreams have died
But life can still be worth living
The echoes of silence replied

Dishes scream for washing
Piled high upon the kitchen sink
Yes, perhaps I'm feeling sad
A little more than I think

Now we have empty rooms
Without those meaningless smiles
Yet the distance between us
Can still be measured in miles

Bed left unmade again
With clothes lying tangled in a heap
It's a picture full of excuses
Looking so drab and cheap

Empty rooms and meaningless smiles
Continue to distort my point of view
As the night outside stirs
Forgotten memories of you

Understanding

Understanding the plain
    and simple truth is the
        hardest task of all
Can we find a single grain
    of sand
        in the desert
Or seek to pass
    through the eye
        of a needle?

If we have faith
    in our own
        ability then
The second most difficult of tasks
    to achieve is the ability to
        disabuse ourselves

Ability should not be judged
    by one's achievements
        nor confused with desire –
It is the means to an end
    not the end in and of
        itself

I cast my eye across the landscape
    seeing things I am
        unable to comprehend
but within my ignorance
    Innocence is protected
        by the desire
to know the answer

Does my ability to understand
    Lead me to question
        what scholars call
The plain and simple
    truth

Baghdad 2004

Your body may have
    rained down
        in a thousand pieces
    as the car bomb exploded,
        the police fled,
    the soldiers cowered,

    but at least
        you died a free
           man

    It wasn't our arrogance,
        or cowboy attitudes
           that poured oil on water,
        lit the flames,
        engulfed a nation;
    blame the enemies
        of democracy
        for that

    With Saddam gone,
        and seeds of democracy
           already tossed into
                the dusty soil,
    the allies are careful
        not to dwell in the past,
           or present;
    they gaze forward to the future

Safely tucked up in their beds
    in London and New York
        it is not they who have
    to bend down and
        pick up the pieces –
the pieces of a man
    who never knew
freedom till he died

LOVE'S KEEPSAKE

All of a Sudden

All of a sudden
I was out of control
You had my body
But longed for my soul

The excitement inside
Started to swell:
Take me to heaven –
Cast me down to hell

You took your pleasure
In my moment of despair
When I looked for comfort
Found none to be there

All of a sudden
I was adrift out at sea
With waves of emotion
Cascading down on me

Morning's cruel light
Sees an empty vessel afloat
In panic I shout
But I find a lump in my throat

Where is the captain,
What happened to the crew?
I lie here feeling wrecked
Completely abandoned by you

Waiting for the Man

I'm stuck here waiting
Just as I've done before
But each time's been a no-show
There's never been a knock on my door
They say expect someone to come
Anytime between one and six
So I'm stuck here waiting
With a problem I can't fix

It's That Time Again

It's that time again
When at the crossroads
I look back at the past
and the footsteps of regret
try desperately hard to
hold me back

It's that time again
When I turn to face
the unknown path
that stretches beyond
the here and now
and find myself frozen
to the spot

LOVE'S KEEPSAKE

It's that time again
When the weight
of the world sits upon
my shoulders
because I believed
you knew me

It's that time again
When all roads lead
back to where it all
began to fall apart
and excuses muffled
the sound of footsteps
taking their leave

Flotsam and Jetsam

Disregarded or discarded?
Thrown overboard or the aftereffect
Of a wreck torn asunder
Washed up on a distant shore

There Was a Time Before You

There was a time before you
Where life and existence rolled on
Unruffled and unchallenged,
Mundane and perfectly safe,
Then you caught hold of me

In the same way tinder responds
To the spark that lights the fire,
Engulfed and consumed
I was transformed within
Lost, yet unbelievably found,
Brought back to life with passion

Grasping a desire to explore
Now I question my existence
Craving a life that twists and turns
In unpredictable ways,
Neither mundane nor safe

There was a time before you
A time that is no more
Because you transformed me
Releasing who I am

LOVE'S KEEPSAKE

There's Nothing

There's nothing quite like the taste
Of salted fish and chips
Or the feeling after that
Long lingering kiss from your lips
There's nothing to compare with hours
Spent engaged in conversation
Or that moment when you
Break through doubts and hesitation
There's nothing I wouldn't give
For the routine of being by your side
To avoid the emptiness felt
When the door shuts and I remain inside

The Things I Do

Instead of counting sheep to go to sleep
I count the times we laughed, behaved daft
When morning wakes me, I hope to be
Talking to you before that first coffee or tea

Hope you don't fear that I want you near
Think there's something wrong; if I come on strong
You reject how it feels and take to your heels
And in an instance create an impossible distance

Thoughts go round and round without a sound
Sometimes I feel insecure, quickly becoming unsure

So tormented by the past, hoping the present will last,
But inside I'm petrified, what if our love died?

Once I'm in bed, I try to deal with what's in my head
I snuggle up warm, seeking calm after the storm
And as I drift away, I hope and I pray, like today
My day starts and ends thinking about my friends

Out of the Blue

There you are, minding your own business,
And suddenly, without warning,
You are caught unaware apart from
Hearing the penny drop, reality striking,
An unexplainable pain in the chest.

Out of the blue:
A sound, an image, words
Bring everything back into focus,
Forcing you to see the heartbreak
You were busily trying to ignore.